One Hundred
Songs
of Toil

COMPILED AND EDITED BY
Karl Dallas

WITH GUITAR CHORDS

WOLFE PUBLISHING LIMITED
10 EARLHAM STREET · LONDON WC2H 9LP

Also by Karl Dallas:

SWINGING LONDON (1967, revised 1968)

SINGERS OF AN EMPTY DAY (1971)

THE CRUEL WARS (1973)

GREAT FOLKSONGS OF OUR TIME (1973)

Also from Wolfe:

THE CRUEL WARS
72340493 3   £1.60

BAWDY BRITISH FOLK SONGS
72340492 5   60p

100 FOLK SONGS AND NEW SONGS
72340049 0   60p

THE TEMPERANCE SONG BOOK
72340486 0   £1.25

BEST IRISH SONGS by Percy French
72340428 3   25p

BEST SONGS AND BALLADS OF OLD
    IRELAND
72340413 5   25p

THE OLD TIME STARS' BOOK OF MUSIC HALL
    AND VARIETY SONGS
72340451 8   £5.00

DEDICATED TO THE MEMORY
OF MY FATHER
STANLEY ERNEST 'JACK' DALLAS
ENGINEER BY TRADE
AND AGITATOR BY CONVICTION
1880–1957

Printed in Great Britain by Halstan & Co. Ltd. Amersham Bucks.

CONTENTS

INTRODUCTION

You won't hear many folk songs being sung on the assembly line at Dagenham or Coventry. It is not so much the noise, for the equally noisy weave-rooms of a hundred years ago produced a fine crop of excellent songs, though loom-minders had to learn lip-reading in order to communicate in the midst of the racket. It is the very nature of the work which makes the motor trade so inimical to folklore, for it is somewhat appropriate that the motor car, which is destroying the cities and countryside of the world with all the reckless abandon of an out-of-control Juggernaut, should have been in the forefront of the destruction of the work process itself, fragmenting it into meaninglessness, alienating the worker from his fellows, from the labour of his hands and, ultimately, from himself.

The subject of industrial folklore is a contentious one among scholars of our traditions. Indeed, a hundred years ago there would have been nothing to discuss: since folklore was defined as the survival of archaic customs into modern times, clearly something as new as the industrial system could have no folklore. The very term 'industrial folklore' would have been regarded as a contradiction in terms not so obvious to this age, which has accepted the equally apparent paradox of industrial archaeology.

What the folklorists of the nineteenth century thought they were documenting were the last vestiges of an ancient but moribund culture, the product of a mythical age before man discovered the poison apple of gold and literacy and fell from his primitive grace. The triumph of industrialism seemed certain and well nigh already absolute, destroying much rural folklore in its progress, and only a few anarchic cranks like William Morris questioned the inevitability of its final victory. The view that folklore was doomed is something that Karl Marx would no doubt have shared with these antiquarian academics if he had thought much about the lifestyle of the oppressed classes whose liberation he was planning on such scientific lines—in one of his rare references to folklore, as such, he describes it as 'the idiocy of rural life' in the *Communist Manifesto*—and it is still the view of a modern seer like Marshall McLuhan that oral folk culture was

11

completely extinguished by the mechanical state structure erected upon the foundations laid by the Gutenberg printing press.

Later research than that of Marx and the nineteenth century folklorists, however, has revealed that the death of the folk community was as exaggerated as Mark Twain's, and it is ironic that it should have been the followers of Marx who showed the community to be in a strong enough state, though co-existing with the industrial system, that they could still, if given the chance, begin the task of re-creating a collective society here and now.

Marx's view of the positive virtue of industrial capitalism in forcing mankind a few steps further along the rocky road to the ultimate of communist society is well known; this was Stalin's justification for the horrors of the forced industrialisation of town and country in the pre-war period, and the reason why Marx himself was so unsympathetic to the machine-wrecking activities of the Luddites, however much he felt for them in their (in his view) inevitable suffering. To his mind, it was the industrial proletariat who would, as a result of the very machinery that oppressed them, be forged by capitalism itself into the instruments of its own destruction.

One consequence of this view of Marx, however, was the growth of a proletarian mystique, especially among the many revolutionaries who were not themselves of proletarian origin. Among such as these, a cult grew up around a romanticised idea of factory workers as opposed to other members of what pre-Marxist reformers would probably have described vaguely as the lower classes, the peasants, artisans and individual craftsmen who were regarded by Marx as the anachronistic survivals of feudalism.

It was this somewhat romanticised view of overall proletarians leaping, spanners and hammers at the ready, straight out of the cartoons in the *Daily Worker* to make the revolution, that created the climate of opinion in which quasi-Marxists like Ewan MacColl and A. L. Lloyd started looking for industrial folksong. It was not a question of whether such a thing was possible, because the prophet of socialist realism, A. A. Zhdanov had already laid it down that there must be a distinct culture of the masses, separate from the kitsch of the popular song as performed on the radio and gramophone record. As Lloyd suggested in his pioneer study of British coal mining songs, *Come All Ye Bold Miners,* the fact that such a body of industrial folklore had not so far been discovered perhaps proved that the folklorists had been too busy in the countryside to research what was happening in the cities.

Though this was true of most early folklorists, as we have seen, it was less than fair to the best of them. Frank Kidson noted examples of song one could certainly categorise as industrial, and while Cecil Sharp had defined folksong as 'peasant song' he hastened to point out that it was not so much the rural milieu as the continued existence of a rural community, its traditions relatively undamaged by literacy, compulsory education, mass communications or the factory system, which created the *sine qua non* for the survival of folklore.

Nevertheless, it was not until the work of MacColl and Lloyd (no doubt inspired by Korson's work among the Pennsylvania miners that had produced his excellent study, *Coal Dust on the Fiddle*, with its many songs obviously stemming from the British Isles) that it began to become obvious that there was indeed a whole corpus of material worthy to be described as industrial folklore.

However, in proving the existence of industrial folklore, the quasi-Marxists had revealed the fact that certain industries were more productive of folklore than others, with coalmining easily leading the field, weaving close behind, some songs coming from the railways, and virtually none from the quintessential capitalist industries such as motor car manufacture. A study of the music of the pubs in the 'Jericho' area of Oxford, patronised by workers from the Morris Cowley Car works, has shown that what traditional music there was in the area came from people who did not work in the car factory. And though the Morris body plant had a flourishing brass band entering for national contests (indeed, the Austin-Morris group still has one), the truly popular street bands that played around 'Jericho' included not a single car worker. Perhaps the very existence of the factory band has been a factor here. Bob Davenport has pointed out the deleterious effect of competition-style brass bands upon the music played at the Durham miners' gala, and the analogous choral movement in Wales is no doubt responsible for the dearth of folksong in that 'land of song', even among the miners.

Where Lloyd and MacColl have recognised this variation from industry to industry they have tended to ascribe it to accident, or to the fact that no one can have looked hard enough in the industries seemingly deficient in folklore, which is why I call them quasi-Marxists, for Marx himself would never have missed the evidence before his eyes so unscientifically.

What appears to me to distinguish those industries rich in folklore from those where it is rare or non-existent is the surviving collective nature of at least a part of the labour process, strongest in the mines even today, despite the National Coal Board's attempts to 'factoryise' them, surviving in cloth weaving for as long as the work retained vestiges of co-operative effort, and dying out as it became more and more fragmented with increasing mechanisation, never strong in railways where the hierarchical cleaner-fireman-driver structure tended to separate the men on the footplate from one another, but surviving in the quite different atmosphere of the engine sheds or off-duty in railway communities like Doncaster or Crewe.

E. P. Thompson has pointed out, in his *Making of the English Working Class* that 'The factory hands, so far from being the "eldest children of the industrial revolution" were late arrivals . . . And in many towns the actual nucleus from which the labour movement derived ideas, organisation, and leadership was made up of such men as shoemakers, weavers, saddlers and harnessmakers, booksellers, printers, building workers, small tradesmen, and the like'.

It was these elements, and the publicans, who supported the handloom weavers and handframe knitters in their hopeless rearguard action to defend their community against the onset of mechanisation, which became known as Luddism. Even the name of their movement points to its being a true folk revolt, for it derives from their mythical leader, Ned Ludd, which reminds us of King Lud, legendary founder of London, who has two pubs and Ludgate Hill named after him. And the prefix 'Lud' which appears in so many place names, is said to derive from a Saxon word 'leod', meaning 'people'.

A handbill found pasted in a Nottingham street on the morning of Saturday May 9, 1812, nobody knew by whom, warned:

Deface this who dare
They shall have Tyrants' fare
For Ned is everywhere
And can see and hear.

Even a cursory reading of the documents of the period, to be found in Aspinall's *The Early English Trade Unions,* shows the solidarity of the community, even extending to some local magistrates. Frank Peel, a Yorkshire journalist who did much painstaking research and took a great deal of oral testimony from former Luddites, wrote: ' . . . the most marvellous thing about the Luddite movement is the manner in which the secrets of the body were kept . . . but they doubtless were well aware that many who did not actually join them, sympathised with the movement to some extent, hoping, unlikely though it seemed, that it would tend in some way towards the amelioration of their own hard lot.'

In fact, it was not 'amelioration' that was their aim, so much as resistance to a process of social change which they felt threatened them and their community.

Thompson says on this: 'A way of life was at stake for the community and, hence, we must see the croppers' opposition to particular machines as being very much more than a particular group of skilled workers defending their own livelihood. These machines symbolised the encroachment of the factory system.' The croppers were men who cut the nap off cloth using huge 40-pound hand shears.

Though the Luddites lost their fight, the principles of solidarity with the remainder of the community persisted in the struggles that were to follow, so excellently documented by Aspinall. A handbill of the Blackburn weavers on strike declared themselves willing 'to enter into subscriptions for the relief of small families, who might in the first instance be hurt by the measure.' This reminds us of the action of the miners in the great strike of 1972 in ensuring that old people in their communities were adequately supplied with coal throughout the stoppage.

The Sheriff of the County of Lanarkshire in 1812 had to warn local inhabitants supporting the striking weavers in Glasgow that their subscriptions 'encourage proceedings illegal in themselves' and that such donations, he implied, were themselves illegal. Nevertheless, as a local man wrote confidentially to the Prime Minister at the time. 'The commonalty of Glasgow support the weavers by credit and by subscription . . . The landed interest rather take their part, and have given them employment in agriculture, to which they resort with pleasure and activity.'

This support of the Scottish landed gentry is interesting, for it may point to a situation analogous to that noted by Engels in Ireland, where the local lords were not so much survivals of the feudal order as of the much older clan system. It is to this old collective that all folk traditions lead us back, as Lewis Henry Morgan suggested in *Ancient Society,* a line of enquiry pursued by Engels so brilliantly in his *Origin of the Family.*

This clannishness—which is what it was, in a very literal sense—is the basis of all the folk tales about villages who had tools, knives, porridge spoons and so on in common. Tacitus reported that this had been the case with the ancient German tribes, and another historian, Cosmas of Prague, reported of his ancestors that 'Like the radiance of the sun, or the wetness of the water, so the ploughed fields and the pastures, yea even the very marriages, were all in common . . .'

As such things do, memories of this state of affairs have become jokes in our time; suggesting that villagers holding tools in common were too poor to afford more than one tool in the village. It is said that the people of Dean Head, near Huddersfield, had holes in the walls of their terrace houses so they could pass a single knife back and forth from one end of the village to the other. Whoever wanted it had to call through the hole for it and the message went down the line, one house to another, until the knife was located. In the village of Cononley, south of Skipton, the same tale is told of a communal frying pan, and for that reason many locals still refer derisively to the main street as Frying Pan Alley. There is a Poggy Tub Row in Otley with a similar reputation (a poggy tub is a washtub). In Netherton, near Huddersfield, it is said that once the three pubs in the village each had a cradle, one large enough for a single child, another large enough for twins, a third for triplets, for use by the poor of the village. Clearly this is a folk memory of an old community feeling when, as the Yorkshire saying has it, if you prick one inhabitant they all bleed.

It was from such clannish villages as these that the strongest opposition to industrialism came.

Though Marx recognised the part that steam-engine technology played in creating capitalist society, he saw the break-up of the folk community that accompanied it as, historically speaking, a progressive step. He did not notice that, even as he wrote, a new kind of technology was emerging that was to make possible the re-creation of the collective, the technology of electronics.

It is interesting that the first attempts to turn factory production back into a co-operative process have been taking place in the electronics industry, with Philips' experiments in Holland with circular production lines, in which every worker can envisage his work as part of a tangible whole, visible in the tape recorder taking shape before his eyes. Interesting, too, that in the very industry which spawned the epitome of fragmented labour, Volvo are experimenting with similar ways of involving the car worker in the overall product of his labour and that first indications are that the experiment is a success in capitalist economics as well as human terms.

It would be valuable if folkorists were to direct their attention to these factories to see if, as I think likely, a flowering of folklore and a community sense result, even though the Volvo experiment is doomed to fail ultimately in a wider sense, as the car becomes a less and less viable means of transport in a society where electronic communication replaces physical travel for all but recreational needs. A recent EEC paper recommended the abandonment of the assembly-line system throughout capitalist Europe — a move that could have far-reaching collectivist effects if implemented.

So far we have spoken as if industrial folksong were all one, but in fact folklorists recognise two kinds of worksong: songs about work (a category which covers almost all the songs in this collection) and songs which have the purpose of assisting the workers to co-ordinate their efforts such as the waulking songs used by Hebridean handloom weavers as they shrink their cloth, sea shanties, chain-gang songs from the American South, Xhosa roadsongs from South Africa, and the like.

In an intriguing early essay, *The part played by labour in the transition from ape to man,* Engels suggested that speech evolved out of the co-ordinated grunting of apes involved in collective effort, and it is this grunting which is at the root of all such worksongs.

When I worked for a while in a circus, our efforts in erecting the Big Top were co-ordinated in this way by the tentmaster shouting a rhythmic 'hah-hah-hah!' with which we all joined. In America, I have heard, there are fully fledged tent-raising shanties, complete with words of verses and choruses, but no one I have spoken to in European circuses has come across any on this side of the Atlantic.

I wonder if Engels' thoughts on the subject were prompted by a discussion in the antiquarian journal, *Notes and Queries*, in the late 1870s on the grunting of 'paviors' who rammed home the paving stones of the London streets.

A Mr Edward Solly reported that 'I have often, between 1820 and 1830, watched London paviors at work and observed that each man as he threw down the ram with a thud at the same time shouted out *hah, hoh, hi* or *huff.* During the last few years, however, I have observed that paviors no longer do this . . .'

Another learned gentleman confirmed this, stating that 'forty years ago one much concerned with such matters told me that a pavior who neglected to groan was "fined a pot" by his comrades.' The reason for the change, he suggested, was technological and I imagine he must have been right.

This is also the reason why there appear to be no worksongs to accompany the labour in modern industry, though worksongs have been sung in the Portland stone quarries as the quarrymen hammer their wedges into the rock as recently as 1950s, and for all I know still are.

The lack of this type of worksong in industry is but further evidence of the anti-social nature of the industrial work process.

About songbooks in general and these songs in particular

Most of the songs in this book came originally from traditional sources and while in many cases I know the singers from whom I got them originally, and can point to songbooks which have published very similar versions (there's a list of songbooks at the end), they have become quite different in the years I've been singing them. Sometimes I have stopped singing them altogether for a while and in order to present a completed text I have had to reconstruct lines or even whole verses to make up for gaps in my memory.

Wherever possible, I have indicated recordings in which versions of the songs may be heard; rarely are the words and music as printed here exactly as you would hear them on such a recording, and that only by accident, often because the recorded singer and I obtained them from the same source. Some of the older and more familiar songs have come from the pioneer folksong collections but since these did not always include music—though they might give the name of the tune—the melody given may not necessarily be that sung originally.

All this is to say that this is not so much a work of folksong scholarship but rather an introduction to a whole corpus of epic and lyric which more and more people are feeling to be an essential hard core to our very essence as human beings. Before I put them in this book I had been singing many of them for years, occasionally in public even since I gave up professional singing, but much more important at home in the family circle, and thus I have made them my own, not by appropriating their copyright, but by singing them and whittling away at them until they fitted me.

You should do the same.

Throughout this book I have attempted to avoid the literary affectation of writing down dialect as if it were a foreign language, which indeed it often thus becomes. I agree with the villagers of whom Alfred Williams wrote in his *Folk Songs of the Upper Thames*: 'The villagers speak dialect but do not care to read it. They are shocked and offended when they see their own language written. The townspeople do not speak dialect, but like to read it. There is the difference.'

Another objection to printed dialect, to which Maxine Baker referred in her unpublished thesis on the miners' songs of Northumberland and Durham, is that it is inconsistent. Where one collector will put 'ah' for 'I', another will put 'aw', and since the original informant was under the impression that he was singing 'I' anyway, the whole thing becomes ridiculous. The only accurate way of rendering dialect is by using phonetics, but even this takes no cognisance of the transitory nature of all human speech, which for instance has banished the Cockney substitution of 'w', for 'v' in the past century, and perpetuates the common folklorist's mistake of seeing folk culture as a thing rather than a process, where change is as significant as preservation.

I am aware that in certain parts of the country, notably Lancashire and Tyneside, print has spawned a local breed of dialect writers whose roots are undeniably in folk traditions. In a future volume I hope to collect together much of this dialect verse and, since the way it looks is an essential part of the form, I shall retain the peculiarities of spelling which are the hallmark of such dialect poets as Samuel Laycock and Joe Wilson. But since these songs are intended to be sung, not merely looked at, I have avoided this as much as possible here.

Only in some original contemporary songs, or when a word is sufficiently different (eg 'gan' for 'go', 'hoo' for 'she') to affect the flavour of the song if changed, or when the whole cadence of the words becomes unbalanced without the dialect usage of, say, 'ye' for 'you', have I left it.

This may offend my friends in Lancashire, my compatriots of Tyneside, and especially the Scottish nationalists, but if it is any consolation to them my sin has been one of commission rather than omission, committed after careful thought.

WORKING LIFE OUT

THE WORKING CHAP

I'm a wor - king chap as you may see, You'll
find an ho - nest lad in me; I'm
nei - ther haugh - ty, mean nor proud, Nor
ev - er takes the thing too rude. I
ne - ver gang a - bune my means, Nor
seek as - sis - tance frae my frien's, But

day and nicht through thick and thin, I'm

work-ing life out to keep life in.

Nae_ mat - ter frien's, what - e'er be - fa', The

poor folks they maun work a - wa', Through

frost and snow and rain and wind, They're

work - ing life out to keep life in.

I'm a working chap as you may see,
You'll find an honest lad in me.
I'm neither haughty, mean nor proud,
Nor ever takes the thing too rude.
I never gang abune my means
Nor seek assistance frae my frien's,
But day and nicht through thick and thin,
I'm working life out to keep life in.

chorus: Nae matter, frien's, whate'er befa',
The poor folks they maun work awa',
Through frost and snow and rain and wind
They're working life out to keep life in.

The poor needlewoman that we saw
In reality and on the wa',
A picture sorrowful to see,
I'm sure with me you'll all agree.
Her pay's scarce able to feed a mouse,
Far less to keep herself and house.
She's naked, hungry, pale and thin,
Working life out to keep life in.

Don't call a man a drunken sot
Because he wears a ragged coat.
It's better far, mind, don't forget,
To run in rags than run in debt.
He may look seedy, very true,
But still his creditors are few,
And he toddles on, devoid of sin,
Working life out to keep life in.

But maybe, frien's, I've stayed ower long,
But I hope I hae said nothing wrong.
I only merely want to show
The way the poor folk have to go.
Just look at a man with a houseful of bairns,
To rear them up it takes all he earns.
With a willing heart and a coat gey thin,
He's working life out to keep life in.

From Ord's pioneer collection of *Bothy Songs and Ballads.* The
bothy was a long low shed used for accommodating workers hired
by the season, mainly in Aberdeenshire. As Hamish Henderson said
in his notes to an excellent album of bothy songs from traditional
singers (Tangent TNGM 109), 'It was the bothy system on North-
east farms which served as a sort of folksong incubator in late-
Victorian and Edwardian days. The unmarried farm labourers were
accommodated in stone-built outhouses called bothies, and they
spent a lot of time making their own music . . .'

THE DUBLIN JACK-OF-ALL-TRADES

I__ am a ro-ving spor-ting blade, they call me Jack-of-all-trades, I al-ways placed my chief de-light in court-ing pret-ty fair maids, So when in Dub-lin I ar-rived to try for a sit-u-a-tion I al-ways heard them say it was the pride of all the na-tions.

CHORUS

I'm a ro-ving Jack-of-all-trades Of ev'-ry trade and all trades, And if you wish to know my name, Then call me Jack-of-all-trades.

I am a roving sporting blade, they call me Jack-of-all-trades,
I always placed my chief delight in courting pretty fair maids,
So when in Dublin I arrived to try for a situation
I always heard them say it was the pride of all the nations.
chorus: I'm a roving Jack-of-all-trades,
            Of every trade and all trades,
            And if you wish to know my name,
            Then call me Jack-of-all-trades.

On George's Quay I first began and there became a porter,
Me and my master soon fell out which cut my acquaintance shorter.
In Sackville Street a pastry cook, in James's Street a baker,
In Cook Street I did coffins make, in Eustace Street a preacher.

In Baggot Street I drove a cab and there was well requited,
In Francis Street had lodging beds and all my friends invited.
For Dublin is of high renown or I am much mistaken,
In Kevin Street, I do declare, sold butter, eggs and bacon.

In Golden Lane I sold old shoes, in Meath Street was a grinder,
In Barrack Street I lost my wife, I'm glad I ne'er could find her.
In Mary's Lane I've dyed old clothes of which I've often boasted,
In that noted place, Exchequer Street, sold mutton ready roasted.

In Temple Bar I dressed old hats, in Thomas Street a sawyer,
In Pill Lane I sold the plate, in Green Street an honest lawyer.
In Plunkett Street sold cast-off clothes, in Bride's Alley a broker,
In Charles Street I had a shop, sold shovel, tongs and poker.

In College Green a banker was, and in Smithfield a drover,
In Britain Street a waiter and in George's Street a glover,
On Ormond Quay I sold old books, in King Street a nailer,
In Townsend Street a carpenter and in Ringsend a sailor.

In Cole's Lane a jobbing butcher, in Dame Street a tailor,
In Moore Street a chandler and on the Coombe a weaver,
In Church Street I sold old ropes, on Redmond's Hill a draper,
In Mary Street sold 'bacco pipes, in Bishop Street a Quaker.

In Peter Street I was a quack, in Greek Street a grainer,
On the harbour I did carry sacks, in Werburgh Street a glazier,
In Mud Island was a dairyboy where I became a scooper,
In Capel Street a barber's clerk, in Abbey Street a cooper.

In Liffey Street had furniture, with bugs and fleas I sold it,
And at the Bank a big placard I often stood to hold it.
In New Street I sold hay and straw and in Spitalfields made bacon,
In Fishamble Street was at the grand old trade of basketmaking.

In Summerhill a coachmaker, in Denzille Street a gilder,
In Cork Street was a tanner, in Brunswick Street a builder,
In High Street I sold hosiery, in Patrick Street sold all blades,
So if you wish to know my name then call me Jack-of-all-trades.

Like many other fine Irish songs (see *The Jolly ploughboy* in *The Cruel Wars* for another example) this is to an English air, first published in Elizabethan times. George Colman wrote his well-known song, *Unfortunate Miss Bailey* (who hanged herself, one morning in her garters) to the same tune. Colm O Lochlainn says these words were popular among Dublin ballad singers in 1912. It's interesting to see how John Hasted adapted some of the ideas (and changed others) for his song of 1955 which follows.

THE STREETS OF LONDON

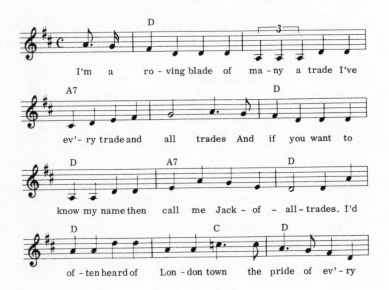

I'm a ro - ving blade of ma - ny a trade I've

ev'- ry trade and all trades And if you want to

know my name then call me Jack - of - all - trades. I'd

of - ten heard of Lon - don town the pride of ev' - ry

na - tion   At   twen – ty   one   it's   here I've come to

try   for   a   sit - u - a - tion.

words: John Hasted

I'm a roving blade of many a trade, I've every trade and all trades,
And if you want to know my name, then call me Jack-of-all-trades.
I'd often heard of London town, the pride of every nation.
At twentyone it's here I've come to try for a situation.

In Covent Garden I began and there I was a porter,
My boss and I we soon fell out which made acquaintance shorter.
Then I drove a number fortysix from Waterloo to Wembley,
Where I became an engineer on aeroplane assembly.

In Charlotte Street I was a chef, in Stepney Green a tailor,
But very soon they laid us off, so I became a sailor.
In Rotherhithe a stevedore, in Gray's Inn Road a grinder,
On Hampstead Heath I lost my wife—it's sad but I never could find
    her.

In Downing Street I was a lord, in Denmark Street I made songs,
In every street and all the streets with my banjo I played songs.
In Harley Street I was a quack, in Turnham Green a teacher,
On Highbury Hill a halfback and on Primrose Hill a preacher.

In Gower Street I'd furniture, with fleas and bugs I sold it,
In Leicester Square a big white car, I often stood to hold it.
By London Bridge I'd lodging beds for all who made their way
    there,
For London is of high renown and Scotsmen often stay there.

I'm a roving blade of many a trade, I've every trade and all trades,
And if you want to know my name, then call me Jack-of-all-trades.

I've tried my hand at everything from herringbones to hatpegs
But I can raise my head and say that I've never been a blackleg.

With this song I break, briefly, one of the rules upon which this collection is based, that every song should be composed by a bona fide worker in the industry concerned, though at the time he wrote it, John Hasted was one of our leading songmakers, pioneer in Britain of the 5-string banjo and 12-string guitar, running a skiffle club in Gerrard Street at which many of the later developments in British popular music, from traditional balladry to rhythm 'n' blues, first got a hearing. The slightly incongruous preachy last line dates it: in these cool commercial days one wouldn't point such an obvious moral. Interesting that in the list of jobs he hasn't actually done, Hasted doesn't mention his true occupation. He is one of Britain's leading physicists and is now a professor at Birkbeck College, London University.

THE ROAMING JOURNEYMAN

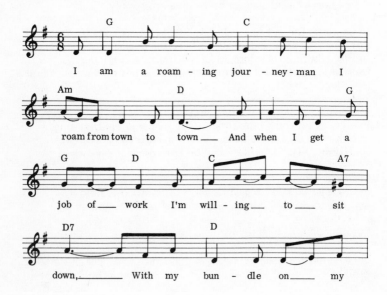

I am a roam - ing jour - ney-man I roam from town to town ___ And when I get a job of ___ work I'm will - ing ___ to ___ sit down, ___ With my bun - dle on ___ my

shoul - der___ and my tro - wel in ___ my hand,_____ And it's round the coun - try I will go like a roam- ing___ jour - ney - man.____

I am a roaming journeyman, I roam from town to town,
And when I get a job of work I'm willing to sit down.
With my bundle on my shoulder and my trowel in my hand,
And it's round the country I will go, like a roaming journeyman.

Now when I get to London town the girls they jump with joy,
Saying one unto the other, Here comes the roaming boy.
One hands to me the bottle while the other holds the can,
And the toast goes round the table, here's good luck to the
        journeyman.

I had not been in London town but one or two days, or three,
Before my master's daughter growed very fond of me.
She asked me in to dine with her, she took me by the hand,
And she slyly told her mammy how she liked the journeyman.

No, hold your tongue dear daughter, how can you say so?
To fall in love with a journeyman you've never seen before.
Oh hold your tongue, dear mammy, I'll do the best I can,
And tomorrow night I'll go to bed along with the journeyman.

I cannot think the reason why my love she looks so sly,
I never had any false heart for any young female kind,
I never had any false heart for any young female kind,
But I always went a-roaming for to leave my girl behind.

The tune is from Tom Willett, a fine didikai singer who was 84 when he recorded it for Paul Carter (to be heard on Topic 12T84). Alas, his sons aren't a patch on him for singing. I have added a couple of verses from the more well-known *Roving journeyman* with the lilting Irish tune so well known in the singing of Delia Murphy and others. Incidentally, it is this tune and not Tom's which is sometimes used for *Down in a coalmine*. Tom used to sing 'with my stick all in my hand' but in many English country versions the travelling man is a stonemason or a bricklayer, hence the trowel.

THE STONECUTTER BOY

A stonecutter boy coming home from his work,
A young damsel appeared in his sight,
Oh, my love, said he, come and sit you down by me,
And I'll tell you what I dreamed about last night,
And I'll tell you what I dreamed about last night.

She stopped and she sighed with a smile on her cheeks,
She stopped and she sighed, saying No.
I am going down for the cow and I cannot stay now,
So I pray you, young man, let me go.

It was they lay down together 'neath a green shady tree,
And this pretty maid she gave a little scream,
And what they done there she never would declare,
But she had the contents of his dream.

Then they both went off together, the cow for to milk,
And so nimbly they tripped o'er the plain.
She said, My dearest dear, the next time that we meet,
You may tell me your dream over again.

As collected by Gardiner from Daniel Wigg of Preston Candover, Alresford, Hants, this was *The bricklayer's dream,* but Lloyd has popularised a three-verse version he calls *The brisk stonecutter boy,* which he has recorded. Ewan MacColl recorded the same one on Argo ZDA 84. This one is something of an amalgam of the two.

THE FACTORY GIRL

As I went a-walking one fine summer's morning,
The birds on the bushes so sweetly did sing.
The lads and the lasses together were sporting
Going down to yon factory their work to begin.

I spied one amongst them was fairer than any,
Her skin like the lily that grows in the dell,
Her cheeks like the red rose that grows in yon valley,
And she's my one only hard-working sweet factory girl.

I stepped up unto her, it was for to view her,
When on me she cast a proud look of disdain.
Stand off me, stand off me, and do not insult me,
For although I'm a poor girl I think it no shame.

I don't mean to harm you nor yet, love, to scorn you,
But grant me one favour, pray where do you dwell?
I am a poor orphan without home or relations
And besides I'm a hard-working factory girl.

I have lands I have houses adorn-ed with ivy,
I have gold in my pocket and silver as well,
And if you'll go with me a lady I'll make you,
So try and say yes, my dear factory girl.

Now love and sensation rules many a nation,
To many a lady perhaps you'll do well.
My friends and my comrades would all frown upon it,
For I'm only a hard-working factory girl.

It's true I did love her but now she won't have me,
And all for her sake I must wander a while
Over high hills and valleys where no one shall know me
Far away from the sound of the sweet factory bell.

I could have printed four or five versions of this widely-spread song; in some of them the girl relents and has the rich young man, in others, as here, no. The first four verses, and tune, here are basically as sung by Mrs Sarah Makem of Keady, Co. Armagh, a place described by Sean O'Boyle as 'a thriving little market town full of tailors and nailers and linen workers'. Mrs Makem is the mother of the more well-known Tommy Makem of Clancy Brothers fame, but a far finer singer, to my mind. The rest of the song is basically as collected by Sam Henry from Mrs Annie Wilson of Moneycannon, who got it from her mother, but I have taken a couple of lines from the singing of Bob Neill, late of Portadown, collected by Robin Morton. Mr Morton is probably right in dating the song from the period when spinning mills were set in rural surroundings to take advantage of water power, but I cannot agree with him that the song is 'an attempt by the folk, still steeped in the old traditions and methods, to understand and control the new, in terms of the known and secure'. You have only to read *My Secret Life* by the anonymous Victorian, Walter, to see how frequently young rich men preyed on working girls, though to judge by Walter's account they were less gallant than appears in the folk narrative. The air sung by Mrs Wilson, by the way, is not dissimilar to that of Margaret Barry's which follows.

THE FACTORY GIRL

As I went out a-walking on a fine summer's morning,
The birds on the bushes would whistle and sing,
The lads and the lassies in couples were sporting,
Going back to the factory their work to begin.

He spied one amongst them, she was fairer than any.
Her cheeks like the red roses that bloom in the spring,
Her hair like the lily that grows in yon valley,
Oh she was only a hard-working factory girl.

He stepped up beside her more closely to view her.
She says, My young man, don't stare me so.
I have gold in my pocket and silver as well.
No more will I answer that factory call.

Though this is clearly a compression of the previous song (despite the rather different ending), the melody as sung by Margaret Barry is so magnificent, that it cannot be left out. Maggie is a gauntly beautiful old lady, now aged 56 or so, with a wild way of singing that is common to the streets of Ireland. She was 12 years old when she set out, on her father's re-marriage, to earn her living singing on the streets to an old zither banjo. She came to England with the great Irish fiddler, Michael Gorman (now dead) in the Fifties, and apart from excursions home and to the United States, she has lived here ever since. No cold print, however, can convey the magnificence of her singing, which you have to go to Topic 12T123 to hear.

THE FACTORY GIRL

words & music: Ralph McTell

Hur-ry-ing a-cross_ the bridge_ Be-fore the si — rens call,_____ This mor-ning she's cha-sing her_ sha-dow_____ All a-long the fac — tor-y wall_____ And thro' the gate_____ where she will wait____ in_

line_____ To cross the yard__
__ to clock her card__ in time__ And
un-der her scarf__ her hair set in curls,__
The day be-gins for the fac-tor-y girl.__

Hurrying across the bridge
Before the sirens call,
This morning she's chasing her shadow
All along the factory wall.
And through the gate where she will wait in line
To cross the yard, to clock her card in time,
And under her scarf her hair set in curls,
The day begins for the factory girl.

For a while the girls try to talk
But their voices soon drown in the din,
And their eyes watch their hands do the work
And a new day's rhythm begins.
No change today, like yesterday the same,
But dinner soon, then afternoon, then home,
Then hurrying home in the fading light
The factory girl is going out tonight.

Her momma says, Don't be late, you've got to get up again
before eight.
Yes, she cries, but there's joy in her eyes as she runs down
the path through the gate.

And out on the rainy streets
Hoping that the night will last
No whispering palms on the beach,
Just the swish of the cars going past.
And she believes no one could feel the same,
Touching and whispering in the rain,
And the rain takes away her beautiful curls,
The night is soon gone for the factory girl.

And hurrying across the bridge
Before the sirens call
This morning she's skipping the puddles
All along the factory wall.
A starling sings, he shakes his wings, she smiles,
Then at the gate she hesitates a while,
Then from inside the gates the sirens roar
And across the yard runs the factory girl.

THE FACTORY GIRL

words & music: Mick Jagger, Keith Richard

1. Wait - ing for a girl who's got
cur - lers in her hair Wait-ing for a
girl who's got no mon-ey a - ny - where
We get bus - es ev - 'ry-where _____

Waiting for a girl who's got curlers in her hair
Waiting for a girl who's got no money anywhere
We get buses everywhere
Waiting for a factory girl.

Waiting for a girl and her knees are much too fat
Waiting for a girl who wears scarves instead of a hat
Her zipper's broken down the back
Waiting for a factory girl.

Waiting for a girl and she gets me into fights
Waiting for a girl, we get drunk on Friday nights
She's a sight for sore eyes
Waiting for a factory girl.

Waiting for a girl and she's got stains all down her dress
Waiting for a girl and my feet are getting wet
She ain't come out yet
Waiting for a factory girl.

© Copyright 1968, 1969 Essex Music International Ltd.

If any folksong purist objects that the two Rolling Stones are hardly folk singers, I would refer him to the discussion of this very point in my *Great Folksongs of Our Time.* However, if you find the constant redefining of definitions among folklorists as tedious as I do, you may only care to acknowledge that there is the same sort of nitty-gritty realism about this lyric that can be found in the best of the nineteenth century ballads, and if we are free of the sentimentalism to be found in many older songs with the same title, I feel this is something of an advance, rather than a loss. Anyone who's stood outside a factory after the going home whistle blows must have seen thousands of girls who fit this description perfectly. The song was recorded by the Stones on what was possibly their greatest album, *Beggars' Banquet.*

THE NAVVY BOY

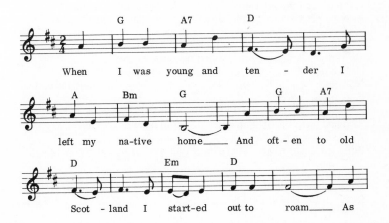

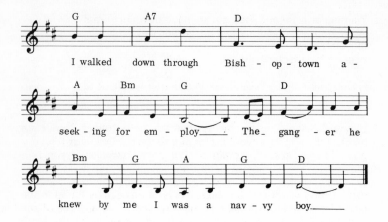

I walked down through Bish - op - town a-seek - ing for em - ploy____ The gang - er he knew by me I was a nav - vy boy.____

When I was young and tender I left my native home
And often to old Scotland I started out to roam.
As I walked down through Bishoptown a-seeking for employ,
The ganger he knew by me I was a navvy boy.

As soon as I did get employ, for lodgings I did seek,
It happened to be that very night with the ganger I did sleep.
He had one only daughter and I became her joy
For she longed to go and tramp with her own dear navvy boy.

Says the mother to her daughter, I think it very strange
That you should wed a navvy boy this wide world for to range.
For navvies they are rambling boys and have but little pay,
How could a man maintain a wife with fourteen pence a day?

Says the daughter to the mother, You need not run them down,
My father was a navvy boy when he came to this town.
He roamed about from town to town just seeking for employ.
Go where he will, he's your love still, he's your own dear navvy boy.

Now just a short time after this her father died, I'm told,
And left unto his daughter five hundred pounds in gold.
And when she got the money, soon I became her joy,
For she longed to go and tramp it with her own dear navvy boy.

Contrary to general belief, the Irish who came to build the English railways and canals, working as navigators or navvies, were not half so wild as the Englishmen they worked beside. Thomas Carlyle wrote in 1846: 'The Yorkshire and Lancashire men, I hear, are reckoned the worst; and not without glad surprise I find the Irish are the best in point of behaviour. The postman tells me that several of the poor Irish do regularly apply to him for money drafts, and send their earnings home.' Many thousands of the 200,000 navvies at one time working were killed, the first of them at Edgehill in August 1827, according to Terry Coleman's *The Railway Navvies.* This song was collected by Sam Henry from Robert J. Lyons of Coleraine and is number 760 in his enormous collection.

BOLD IRISH NAVVY

Oh, I'm a bold Irish navvy that fought on the line,
The first place I met was Newcastle-on-Tyne.
I've been tired, sick and weary from working all day,
To a cot down by the hillside I'm making my way.

Oh I first had my supper and shaved off my beard,
For courting this fair maid I highly prepared.
Stars shone in the sky and the moon it shone down
And I hit for the road with my navvy boots on.

I knocked at my love's window, my knock she did know,
And out of her slumber she wakened so slow.
I knocked there again, and she said, Is that John?
And I quickly replied, With my navvy boots on.

Oh she opened the window and then let me in,
'Twas into her bedroom she handed me then.
The old night being cold and the blankets they rolled down,
So I slept there all night with my navvy boots on.

Oh then early next morning at the dawn of the day,
Said I to my true love, It's time I was away.
Sleep down, sleep down, you know you've done wrong,
For to sleep here all night with your navvy boots on.

Oh he bent down his head with a laugh and a smile,
Saying, What could I do love, in that length of time?
And I know if I done it, I done it in fun,
And I'd do it again with my navvy boots on.

Well, six months being over and seven at the least,
This pretty fair maid she got stout round the waist,
Then eight months being over and nine comes along
And she handed me a baby with his navvy boots on.

Now before the month was over I was brought up to court,
And tried as a sinner as everyone knows,
Tried as a sinner for having done wrong,
But I slept there all night with my navvy boots on.

Oh I hung down my head being unable to speak,
And the magistrate said, You'll pay ten bob a week.
Ten bob a week for a poor farmer's son,
I cursed the first day I put navvy boots on.

So come all you pretty fair maids a warning take by me,
Don't ever let a navvy get into your bed,
For when he'll get warm and think upon yon,
Sure he'll jump on your bones with his navvy boots on.

Most occupations have their own versions of this song (for instance, the miners; see *With my pitboots on*) and the navvy version is as widespread, seemingly, as the railways and canals they navigated through the land. The words don't change much. As I first got it from Fred McKay it was almost identically the same as sung by the Belfast tinker lady, Lal Smith, on Topic 12T158. The two verses about being sued for maintenance were collected by Russell Quay and Hylda Sims in the Queens Arms, South Norwood. When I was in the circus we had a fair number of labourers on the run from maintenance orders.

HOT ASPHALT

Good eve-ning all my joll-y lads I'm glad to see you well, If you gath-er all a-round me boys a stor-y I will tell For I've got a sit-u-a-tion and be-gorr-a and be-gob I can whis-per I've a week-ly wage of nine-teen bob. So you may talk a-bout your

sol - diers and your sai - lors and the rest___ Your tai - lors and shoe-ma - kers who can please the la - dies best. But the dev-il a one of them has got their flin - ty hearts to melt. Like the boys a-round the boil - er stirr - ing hot as - phalt.___

Good evening all my jolly lads, I'm glad to see you well,
If you gather all around me boys, a story I will tell.
For I've got a situation and, begorra and begob,
I can whisper I've a weekly wage of nineteen bob.

chorus: So you may talk about your soldiers and your sailors and
the rest,
Your tailors and shoemakers who can please the ladies
best.
But the devil a one of them has got their flinty hearts to
melt
Like the boys around the boiler stirring hot asphalt.

It's lately gone six months ago since I came to Dublin town
When I helped my Uncle Barney for to cut the harvest down.
But now I wear a guernsey and around my waist a belt,
I'm the gaffer o'er the boys who lay the hot asphalt.

Now one day a peeler comes to me and says he to me, McGuire,
Will you kindly let me light my dúidin at your boiler fire.
So he turns up to the boiler with his coat-tails up so neat.
Now says I, My decent man you better go and mind your beat.
Ah sure, says he, that'll do for me, for I'm up to all your pranks,
And I know you for a traitor from the Tipperary ranks.
Now I threw out from my shoulder and I gave him such a pelt
That I knocked him into the boiler full of hot asphalt.

Well we quickly pulled him out again and threw him in the tub
And with soap and warm water how we did rub and scrub.
But the devil a bit of tar came off, it was stuck on just like stone,
And every rub that we did give, you could hear the peeler groan.

With the rubbing and the scrubbing sure he caught a blooming
        cold
And for scientific purposes his body has been sold.
And now in the national museum, he is hanging by the belt
As a monument to the dire effects of hot asphalt.

A vicious little song with more than a touch of the stage Irish
about it, though the fiery nature of the Celtic temperament was
documented as far back as Caesar and Tacitus. Perhaps it was they
started the legend, if a legend it be. Most of these words are from
the singing of John McLaverty of Belfast, collated with words
noted down by Ewan MacColl from Baldy Thomson, a Dundee
railwayman, and his father, William Miller, of Stirling. The great
Irish singer, piper and collector, Seumas Ennis, has a fine version of
his own, and he must have been startled to hear it sung by Ben
Baxter of Southrepps in the heart of Norfolk in 1956. Or perhaps
not; England is full of Irish songs spread by itinerant workers. A
dúidin (pronounced doo-jeen) is a little clay pipe. The third verse
of eight lines uses the 4-line melody twice.

THE JOLLY GRINDER

tune: *The jolly miller*

There was a jolly grinder once lived by the River Don,
He worked and sang from morn to night, and sometimes he
worked none.
But still the burden of his song for ever used to be:
'Tis never worthwhile to work too long for it doesn't agree
with me!

He seldom on a Monday worked except near Christmas Day.
It was not the labour that he'd shun for it was easier far than play.

But still the burden of his song for ever used to be:
'Tis never worthwhile to work too long for it doesn't agree
    with me!

A pale teetotaller chanced to meet our grinder one fine day
As he sat at the door with his pipe and his glass and thus to our
    friend did say:
You destroy your health and senses too. Says the grinder, You're
    much too free.
Attend to your work, if you've ought to do, and don't interfere
    with me.

There's many like you go sneaking about persuading beer drinkers
    to turn.
'Tis easier far on our failings to spout than by labour your living
    to earn.
I work when I like and I play when I can and I envy no man I see,
Such chaps as you won't alter my plan for I know what agrees
    with me.

Though the broadside in Sheffield City Library from which this comes is undated, it can't be older than 1833 when the term 'teetotal' was coined. The tune, of course, is familiar to most schoolchildren. It was used for a thieves' song in the obscure canting dialect, *The budgeon is a delicate trade,* printed in a collection of 1725, though the 'miller on the Dee' words were found written on the fly-leaf of a volume printed in 1716. A major version of the tune was used for a harvest-supper song, *Here's a health unto our master,* collected by the Rev. John Broadwood. The tune is one of those harmonised by Beethoven in 1824.

CHARLES DOCHERTY

Oh, my name is Charles Doc-her-ty and Rotherham's my
town, You'll see work from my steel mill the
whole world a - round, To en - joy such hard
la - bour I'd hard - ly pre - tend, On a
day in Sept - em - ber I met my cruel end.

Oh, my name is Charles Docherty and Rotherham's my town.
You'll see work from my steel mill the whole world around.
To enjoy such hard labour I'd hardly pretend.
On a day in September I met my cruel end.

That day in the steel-mill the ingot-bloom stuck.
I had to crawl under in the heat and the muck.
But the cause of the stoppage I just couldn't see
So I lit some oil waste to throw light on the scene.

Now the waste it flared up in a shower of flame
And the oil on my overalls it flared up the same.
Oh save me, my workmates, I'll perish indeed
Unless you come help me at the best of your speed.

At the inquest they blamed me for lighting that waste,
They said I could have avoided those perils I faced.
But the hand-lamp being awkward and to move the work on
I laid down my life, my boys, and met my fatal doom.

Now your civilisation is built upon steel,
It's found in each nation, in girder and wheel.
As you ride across rivers and sail in the sea,
Spare a thought, say a prayer, for the steelmen like me.

I heard this song in a working men's club on the outskirts of
Sheffield, but wasn't able to note down either words or tune until
much later. I never found out who composed the song, and my
memory was at fault in several cases where I filled out the lines
myself. I was told at the time it was a true story and the man's
widow received no compensation because the accident was his own
fault.

NAE WARK

words: Joe Wilson

tune: *Pretty Polly Perkins of Paddington Green*

worn out and sair. What_ wretch - ed - ness, what mis - er - y, There's no one can tell, Ex - cept them that's been out of wark like my - sel'.

I's weary, I's wretched, I wander forlorn,
I sigh for the neet and then wish for the morn.
For neet brings nae comfort, and morn little mair,
In both mind and body I's worn out and sair.
chorus: What wretchedness, what misery,
There's no one can tell,
Except them that's been out of wark, like mysel'.

I wander to places and try to get wark,
Where, Call back again is the foreman's remark.
Thus hopeless and cheerless I pass many a day,
Though the pay-week comes round it to me brings no pay.

Nae wark yet, heart-broken I bend my ways hame.
Nae wark yet, to tell them I really think shame,
For dependence is painful, though it's on your own,
Though to comfort and cheer you they try all they can.

There's none can imagine the anguish I feel
When I sit down at hame to my poor humble meal.
Each bite seems to choke us, the day seems full long,
And all that I do, why, I feel that 'twas wrong.

My father looks dull, though he strives to look glad,
And tells us it's nowt to the troubles he's had.
My mother smiles kindly, though sad like the rest.
She whispers, Cheer up lad, and hope for the best.

It cannot last always, I hope afore lang,
With work I'll be freed from sad poverty's pang.
For without it hame's dreary, the fire's bright spark
Turns gloomy and dim when at hame there's nae wark.

The Tyneside comedian Joe Wilson was a printer by trade, the son of a joiner and a straw-bonnet maker, who published his first book when he was 17, went into business on his own account as a printer when he was 21, and was later a local publican. Later, however, he became an advocate of temperance, and wrote a number of songs on the subject. His best-known songs were probably *I wish your mother would come* and *Geordie, haud the bairn.* He died in 1875, aged 33.

WILLIAM BROWN

tune: *In and out the windows*

A nice young man was Will - iam Brown, He
worked for a wage in a north - ern town, He
worked from six 'til eight at night,
Turn - ing a wheel from left to right.
Keep that wheel a - turn - ing,

Keep that wheel a-turn-ing, Keep that wheel a-
turn-ing. And do a lit-tle more each day.

A nice young man was William Brown,
He worked for a wage in a northern town.
He worked from six 'til eight at night,
Turning a wheel from left to right.
chorus: Keep that wheel a-turning,
Keep that wheel a-turning,
Keep that wheel a-turning
And do a little more each day.

The boss one day to William came
And said, Look here young what's-your-name,
We're not content with what you do,
So work a little harder or out you go.

So William turned and he made her run
Three times round in the place of one.
He turned so hard he soon was made
The Lord High Turner of the trade.

William turned with the same sweet smile,
The goods he made grew such a pile
They filled the room and the room next door
And overflowed to the basement floor.

The nation heard the wondrous tale,
The news appeared in the *Sketch* and *Mail*.
The railways ran excursions down
And all to see young William Brown.

But sad the sequel is to tell,
He turned out more than the boss could sell,
The market slumped and the price went down:
Seven more days and they sacked young Brown.

Seldom has the classic Marxian theory of surplus value been better or more succinctly put. Some anonymous member of the Co-op 'scout' movement, the Woodcraft Folk, made it up before World War II, when the process could be seen operating in human terms, in the shutdowns on Jarrow and Clydeside, and the dole queues outside the labour exchanges. Productivity alone is no solution to our economic problems.

THE STRIKE

words: Joe Wilson
tune: *The Gallowgate lad*

Come my can - ny Tyne - si - ders and lis - ten Tiv a song that I's cer - tain you'll like, And I'll whis - per a word kind and chee - ring To the ma - ny poor fel - lows on strike. Let them keep up their hearts as they have done, There's a day for the true and the

brave, And the time 'll yet come when great mas-ters Will find out a me-chan-ic's no slave.

Come my canny Tynesiders and listen
Tiv a song that I's certain you'll like,
And I'll whisper a word kind and cheering
To the many poor fellows on strike.
Let them keep up their hearts as they have done,
There's a day for the true and the brave,
And the time'll yet come when great masters
Will find out a mechanic's no slave.

Is nine hours an unreasonable movement?
Is't not plenty for labour to men?
Let them that condemn't have a try on't
And see if they'll alter such plan.
And if long hours industry increases,
Have they found it with them that they've tried?
With their capital have they got labour
Like that frae the men they've defied?

But a day'll soon come when they'll welcome
The old hands they've so often employed,
Then the foreigners' strength'll be shaken
Frae license that they've long enjoyed,
In making theirsel's their own masters
And working just when they'd a mind.
If the masters pretend to be blind to't,
Whey, it's mair to their shame, that they'll find.

But cheer up, there's good friends that support us,
Aye, and England depends on us a',
And we'll prove that we're true to the movement,
And victory shall let the world know
That Tyneside'll never be conquered
With masters that care nowt for them.
And if masters is meant to be masters
Let them find there's men meant to be men!

The original copy of these words carries the superscription: 'A new song, written expressly for the GREAT CONCERT IN THE NEW TOWN HALL, Monday, September 18th, 1871.' The occasion was presumably in support of the strike at W. Armstrong's engineering works (the 'Armstrong's factory' of *Blaydon races*) for a nine-hour day.

THIS AFTERNOON'S ALL MINE

words & music: Derrek White

Clocked in this morn - ing,___ just in ___
time, and the work was so bor - ing on the
mass pro - duc - tion line, Thro' the dir - ty win-dows I could
see the sun__ shine, And lean-ing on the clock fing-ers,___
You know how it slows___ the time.___ You won't be
see - ing me___ this aft - er noon,___ I

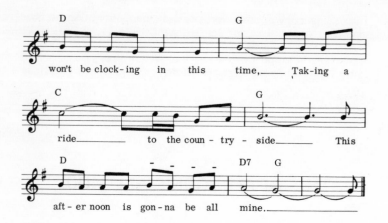

won't be clock-ing in this time,___ Tak-ing a
ride___ to the coun - try - side___ This
aft - er noon is gon - na be all mine.___

Clocked in this morning just in time,
And the work was so boring on the mass production line.
Through the dirty windows I could see the sun shine
And leaning on the clock fingers, you know how it slows the time.
　　You won't be seeing me this afternoon,
　　I won't be clocking in this time.
　　Taking a ride to the countryside.
　　This afternoon is gonna be all mine.

Soon I was on a bus, my dinner upon my knee,
The town behind my shoulders and the hills they were before me.
Highlands and the moorlands, rivers and the sea,
Lancashire has them all to give, all to give for free, to me.

Sometimes a man must stand aside,
Relieve the pressures of trying to survive.
I take to the country, try to ease my mind,
Stand outside my body, take a good look at my life.
　　You won't be seeing me this afternoon,
　　I won't be clocking in this time.
　　Taking a ride to the countryside.
　　This afternoon's gonna be all mine.

I'll never be a British workman, conscientious every day.
I'm such a lousy capitalist, 'cause I love to spend my pay.
Clocked in next morning just in time.
The work was still rolling along the mass production line.

© Copyright 1972

Since he wrote this song, Derrek White has left the factory—he hopes for good—and has been working at various jobs, filling in the gaps in the income he can make singing in folk clubs in the evening. As he put it in a song he wrote at the time:

Think I'll travel to a country place,
Where there's fruit to pick and the air is clean.
Getting industrialised in my brain,
I'm leaving the factory once again.
I think it's time for me to make a move.

You don't get many platitudes about the dignity of industrial labour from the poor buggers who have to do it, day in, day out!

PARODIES

The extent of the use which the folk make of the device of parody in the creation of new songs is something often neglected by folklorists, presumably because rarely do they employ any of the melodies which have been accepted into the canon of folksong. This neglect is a pity, because thus they cut themselves off from one of the most vigorous strains in our folk culture, to be found in almost every walk of life. But nowhere, with the possible exception of the inmates of our prisons and armed forces and schools, does the art flourish so brilliantly as in industry.

Not all songs set to established tunes can be categorised as parodies, of course, even when they retain vestiges of the original. Tommy Armstrong's songs, for instance, stand on their own as compositions in their own right, while a true parody requires the double layer of the old song remembered in the new, the slightly blurred image of two separate stories combining to create a third totality.

This may be why so few folk tunes have been employed, because a really good parody will destroy all reverence for the original, and to the folk these songs are often regarded as sacred, in a quite literal sense. It appears to be only since the folk club movement has created a new category of song which is formally folk but which functions as pop song does, that true parodies of folk songs have begun to appear, like Jack Elliott's upon that now almost hackneyed night visiting song, *The grey cock:*

Wake up, wake up my love, we've slept the clock through,
The bus has flown, the men are gone.
And didn't he glower as he turned ower?
You bloody fool, he said, it's Sunday morn.

As I've said, the tune is hackneyed, and perhaps this is a prime requirement of a parody, not merely because it is essential that all who hear it recognise it immediately, but because it must also have become so familiar that it is no longer treated with any respect. One is not surprised to hear strikers bawling out *We all live on bread and margarine* to the tune of the Beatles' *Yellow submarine,* but a similar parody of, say, *Eleanor Rigby* would be unthinkable.

Thus, a study of parodies tells us something important about the popular songs of the day which is inaccessible to us in any other way. For instance, I would not have thought the songs of Stephen Foster were so well-known a hundred years ago had I not come across this, to the tune of *My old Kentucky home* and dating from the Lancashire cotton famine during the American Civil War:

> *Let us pause in life's pleasures and count its many tears*
> *While we all sup sorrow with the poor.*
> *There's a song that will linger for ever in our ears,*
> *Oh short time, come again no more.*
>
>> *It's the song of the factory operatives:*
>> *Short time, short time, come again no more.*
>> *For we can't get our cotton from the old Kentucky shore,*
>> *Oh short time, short time come again no more.*

From a slightly later period, to the tune of *I wouldn't leave my little wooden hut* is this, collected by Monica Taylor from an old mill-worker of Haslingden, Lancs:

> *I wouldn't leave my two little looms for you,*
> *I've got one Dobbie and I don't want two.*
> *For the weft I weave is as sweet as sugar*
> *And the tackler I work for is a right old bugger,*
> *I wouldn't leave my two little looms for you.*

Probably this was not written by an industrial worker, and the choice of a tune like *There is a tavern in the town* suggests to me a university graduate rather than an engineer as the author, but he could have been a proletarian product of Ruskin:

> *There is a factory in the town*
> *Where belts and cranks move up and down.*
> *With that dull life I never did agree:*
> *Fifty hours of that's enough for me.*

One could go on and on, there are such riches, and in fact the thought strikes me that this may be another reason the field has been neglected: simply that once you have turned on the tap it is hard to turn it off again. One can merely take an arbitrary decision that one has quoted sufficient to make one's point and then, before printing a few that stand up as complete songs, finish up with a final sample like this Durham miners' verse, to the tune of *Moonlight bay*:

> *I was ganning inbye on the engine plane,*
> *I could hear the putter shouting, I'm off the way.*
> *Hawhey give us a lift, my arse is sair.*
> *If I had this tub put I would put nae mair.*

THE BOLD ENGINEERS

words: Wal Hannington
tune: *Bless 'em all*

Now this is the tale of the bold engineers
Who asked for a fifteen bob rise.
They said, Let's be moderate, we won't ask too much,
The public will sympathise.
We waited three months and the boss then replied,
We won't meet your claim in full.
Let this be a caution, we'll give you a portion,
So cheer up my lads, bless 'em all.
chorus: Bless 'em all, bless 'em all,
   The long and the short and the tall.
   Bless all the guv'nors, the shareholders too,
   Managers, foremen and their blinking crew.
   We're saying goodbye to them all,
   We've answered a union call.
   They'll get no production, we've started a ruction,
   So cheer up my lads, bless 'em all.

The forty-hour week is the AEU's claim
But the boss says he won't stand for that.
The early trade unionists started that game
But he's found a way to come back.
He now pays a rate upon which we can't live
So we have to work overtime.
He's scotched our ambition with hours in addition,
So cheer up my lads, let 'em blind.

Now what do we think of the non-union bloke
Who takes all and still won't pay?
He suffers from jitters when he sees the boss
Coming along his way.
In contrast the union man stands erect
And fights for his mates when they call.
He stands by the banner
And hits like a hammer,
So cheer up my lads, bless 'em all.

Wal Hannington first came to prominence during the hungry
Thirties as organiser of the unemployed workers and leader of the

Hunger Marches, but when he wrote this in the Fifties he was an organiser for the Amalgamated Engineering Union. The tune is an old army song.

THE BROO ROAD

tune: *Bye-bye blackbird*

chorus: Oh we're the lads frae the top of the hill,
We never worked and we never will.
We're on the broo road.
Just like the lads frae Peddie Street,
Mention work and we tak oor feet.
We're on the broo road.

Oh then I got a job at the Canby canning herrin'
And I sang a song aboot Maggie hae'in' a bairn.
But the gaffer didnae like my song,
The job didnae rin for long.
Bye-bye canneries.

And then I got a job at the spinning
But when I saw the frames I started rinning.
We're all the same up top of the hill,
Show us a tool and we rin like hell,
Bye-bye spinneries.

And then I got a job with Grant, the bookie,
Collecting tickets at the bottom of St Roukie.
But I gi'ed my clients o'er much sub,
I drank the rest in Johnnie Groat's pub.
Bye-bye bookie.

I know very little about this song except that it is said to have been composed in Dundee during the depression. The broo (or bureau) is an archaic name for the labour exchange, where the unemployed line up for their dole money every week. The song was included by John A. Brune in his collection, *The Roving Songster* (1965).

HEROES OF THE LINE

PADDY WORKS ON THE RAILWAY

In eigh - teen hun-dred and for - ty - one My cor - du - roy bree - ches I put on, My cor - du - roy bree - ches I put on To

CHORUS

work up - on the rail - way. I was wear - ing cor-du-roy bree-ches, Dig - ging dit - ches, dodg - ing hi - tches, pul - ling swit - ches. I was work - ing on the rail - way._____

In eighteen hundred and fortyone
My corduroy breeches I put on,
My corduroy breeches I put on
To work upon the railway.
chorus: I was wearing corduroy breeches,
            Digging ditches, dodging hitches, pulling switches,
            I was working on the railway.

In eighteen hundred and fortytwo
From Hartlepool I went to Crewe
And found myself a job to do
A-working on the railway.

In eighteen hundred and fortythree
I broke my shovel across my knee
And went to work for the company
On the Leeds and Selby Railway.

In eighteen hundred and fortyfour
I landed on the Liverpool shore.
My belly was empty, my hands were sore
With working on the railway.

In eighteen hundred and fortyfive
When Daniel O'Connell he was alive,
When Daniel O'Connell he was alive
And working on the railway.

In eighteen hundred and fortysix
I changed my trade to carrying bricks,
I changed my trade to carrying bricks
From working on the railway.

In eighteen hundred and fortyseven
Poor Paddy was thinking of going to heaven,
Poor Paddy was thinking of going to heaven
From working on the railway.

These are some of the verses Ewan MacColl collected, but there are lots of others. He usually alternates a slow 6/8 verse with two verses in a fast 2/4, but I have stuck to the latter. If you know better verses, or can make up your own, feel free to do so.

THE IRON HORSE

by Charles Balfour

Come, Hie-land-men, come Low-land men, come ev-ery man on earth, man, And I'll tell you how I got on a-tween Dun-dee and Perth, man. I gaed up-on an ir-on road, a rail they did it ca', man, And drag-git by an ir-on horse, an aw-ful beast to draw, man.

Come Hielandmen, come Lowlandmen, come every man on earth, man,
And I'll tell you how I got on atween Dundee and Perth, man.
I gaed upon an iron road, a rail they did it ca', man,
And draggit by an iron horse, an awful beast to draw, man.

Then first and foremost, near the door, there was a wee bit wicket,
It was there they gar'd me pay my ride and they gi'ed me a ticket,

I gaed awa up through the hoose, sat down upon a kist, man,
To tak a look on all I saw on the great big iron beast, man.

There was hooses in a long straight row, a-standing upon wheels,
    man,
And then the chiels that fed the horse were black's a pair of de'ils,
    man.
And ne'er a thing they gave the brute but only coals to eat, man,
He was the queerest beast that e'er I saw for he had wheels for
    feet, man.

A chap cam up and roond his cap he wore a yellow band, man.
He bade me gang and tak my seat, says I, I'd rather stand, man.
He speered if I was going to Perth, says I, And that I be, man,
But I'm weel enough just where I am, because I want to see, man.

He said I was the greatest fool that e'er he saw on earth, man,
For 'twas just the hooses on the wheels that gaed from this to
    Perth, man.
And then he laughed and wondered how I hadnae mair discernment.
Says I, The ne'er a ken kent I, I thought the whole concern went.

The beast it roared and off we gaed, through water, earth, and
    stanes, man,
We ran at sic a fearful rate, I thought we'd brak oor banes, man.
Till by and by we stoppit at a place called something Gowrie,
But ne'er a word had I to say, but only sit and glower, aye.

Then after that we made a halt and in comes Yellow Band man,
He asked me for the ticket and I all my pouches fand, man.
But ne'er a ticket I could get, I'd tint it on the road, man,
So he gar'd me pay for't ower again, or else gang off to quod,
    man.

Then after that we crossed the Tay and landed into Perth, man,
I vow it was the queerest place that e'er I saw on earth, man,
For the hooses and the iron horse were far aboon the land, man,
And hoo they got them up the stairs I canna understand, man.

But noo I'm safely landed and my feet are on the sod, man.
When I gang to Dundee again I'll tak another road, man.
Though I should tramp upon my feet till I'm no fit to stand man,
Catch me again when I'm ta'en in wi' a chap in a yellow band,
    man.

Charles Balfour was stationmaster at Glencarse and first sang this at
a 'festival of railway servants' in 1848, according to Robert Ford,

who included it in his *Vagabond Songs and Ballads of Scotland*. The story of a yokel believing the entire station would transport him to his destination was, Mr Balfour maintained, based on fact. Ewan MacColl found the song still being sung in Dundee loco shed.

COSHER BAILEY

Cosher Bailey had an engine, it was always needing mending,
And according to her power she could do four mile an hour.
chorus: Did you ever see, did you ever see,
            Did you ever see such a funny thing before?

On the night run up from Gower she went twenty mile an hour,
As she whistled through the station, man she frightened half the
        nation.

Cosher bought her second-hand and he paint her up so grand,
When the driver went to oil her, man she nearly bust her boiler.

Oh the sight it was heart-rending, Cosher drove his little engine,
And he got stuck in the tunnel and went up the blooming funnel.

Cosher Bailey's sister Dinah, she was living up in Blaena,
She could knit or darn our stockings but her cooking it was
        shocking.

Cosher Bailey went to Oxford for to pass matriculation,
But he saw a pretty barmaid and he never left the station.

Now Cosher Bailey he did die, and they put him in a coffin,
But one night they heard some knocking — Cosher Bailey only
        joking.

Well the devil wouldn't have him, and it really was no wonder,
So he sent him back to earth to start a hell upon the Rhondda.

Every rugby fan knows the tune and at least some of these verses,
as well as others which are hardly appropriate to our subject. But
Cosher was a real man, a Monmouth ironmaster who built the Taff
Vale railway in 1846. Apparently, the verse about him getting
stuck in the tunnel is based on fact, despite its erotic implications.

MOSES OF THE MAIL

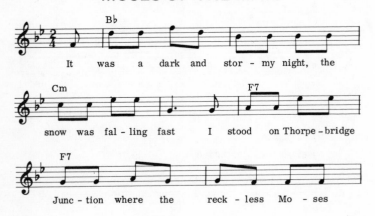

It was a dark and stor - my night, the
snow was fal - ling fast I stood on Thorpe - bridge
Junc - tion where the reck - less Mo - ses

passed His hair was wil - dly wa - ving as through the air he sped, He'd ne - ver had such do - ings since he star - ted at the shed.

LAST VERSE

But when I'm dead and laid to rest, place on my grave sweet ro - ses! These were, I'm told, the ve - ry last ___ path - et - ic words of Mos - es.

It was a dark and stormy night, the snow was falling fast,
I stood on Thorpebridge Junction where the reckless Moses passed.
His hair was wildly waving as through the air he sped.
He'd never had such doings since he started at the shed.

The signals set at Newton Heath, the shed was close at hand.
He sent his mate for some more oil and a couple of bags of sand.
At Moston's dreary cutting the struggle was extreme,
Both front tenders failed to work and the engine wouldn't steam.

On passing Hopwood cabin he heard the engine groan
And reaching for the tallow-pot he broke his collar-bone.
When Castleton appeared in view he shook his weary head
And stepping over to his mate, this is what he said.

I've worked upon the L. and Y. for forty years or more,
But such a wretched night as this I've never had before.
At Hebden Bridge they stopped the train some wagons to re-load
And Moses shouted to his mate, We're off the blooming road.

Up came old Moses, stick in hand, his head hung down with grief.
He viewed the scene contemptuously and then wired for relief.
Pray don't lay violent hands on me, poor Valentine did exclaim,
I know you've done your very best, I know you're not to blame.

The flowers may bud and bloom in spring, and memories fade away,
But they will not forget that night until their dying day.
But when I'm dead and laid to rest place on my grave sweet roses,
These were, I'm told, the very last pathetic words of Moses.

About all that emerges clearly from this rather confused narrative
is the larger-than-life figure of Moses, alias Henry Poyser, engine-
driver on the Manchester to Warrington run in the 1880s, according
to Ewan MacColl who collected three different fragments of song
in Newton Heath loco shed, Manchester and assembled them
together. He recorded the song on Topic 12T104.

A-WORKING ON THE RAILWAY

by Jim Ward

On leav - ing school_ when I was a
lad, To work at a trade_ the same as my
dad. It was the on - ly job to be

had,__ A - work - ing on the rail - **way.**

Too - ra - loo - ra too - ra - li - ay

Work-ing long hours__ for ver - y low pay.

Too - ra - loo - ra - too - ra li - ay__ A -

work - ing on the rail - way.

On leaving school when I was a lad
To work at a trade the same as my dad,
It was the only job to be had,
A-working on the railway.
chorus: Toora-loora, toora-li-ay,
  Working long hours for very low pay.
  Toora-loora, torra-li-ay,
  A-working on the railway.

My carman would harness the horse in his stall.
I couldn't help him because I was small.
Then came the day I was doing it all,
A-working on the railway.

I put on the collar and tighten the ains,
His pad and back-strap, unravel the chains,
The bridle and bit, and fasten the reins,
A-working on the railway.

I sat at the back of a single-horsevan,
That's how my life on the railway began,
Guarding the goods and the load on the van,
A-working on the railway.

From eighteen to twenty, down Billingsgate,
Unloading the fish, the plaice, cod and skate,
Getting my clothes in a terrible state,
A-working on the railway.

Now I'm a carman I'll try to be kind
And smile at the boy who is sitting behind,
My very first day recalling to mind,
A-working on the railway.

I first met Jim Ward in Cecil Sharp House, headquarters of the English Folk Dance and Song Society, ransacking the song files there for songs about the railways, his old employers. He has also researched in the British Museum and the files of trade union journals but he says, sadly, that he hasn't found many. He worked on the horse vans from 1925 to 1931, became a carriage cleaner and eventually ran the staff canteen at Bishopsgate until the station was destroyed by fire. He was retired early because of asthma. He says a lot of ex-delivery men suffer from chest complaints, early victims of pollution.

THE FIREMAN'S GROWL

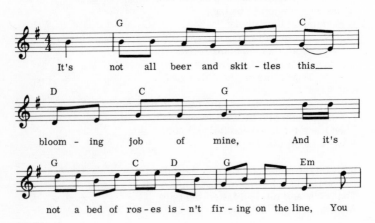

It's not all beer and skit - tles this__ bloom - ing job of mine, And it's not a bed of ros - es is - n't fir - ing on the line, You

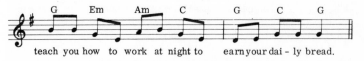

don't get too much mon-ey, you get lots of slack in-stead And they teach you how to work at night to earn your dai - ly bread.

It's not all beer and skittles this blooming job of mine,
And it's not a bed of roses, isn't firing on the line.
You don't get too much money, you get lots of slack instead
And they teach you how to work at night to earn your daily bread.

Just fancy being knocked up in the middle of the night
With a noise enough to wake the dead, give the neighbourhood a
    fright.
You leave your bed with sad regret, prepare to catch your train,
Then a chap comes round to tell you you can go to sleep again.

And when you do get to the sheds, that's when the fun begins
For someone's pinched your spanners and lamps and other things.
You know it's not quite up to Rules, still you like to do the same,
So you take someone else's and pretend you've played the game.

You often get an engine that is very shy for steam
And it's then you start to realise that life's not quite a dream.
You get quite a fed-up feeling when the driver tells you that
We're losing time and then you lose your temper and your hat.

It's lively in the tunnels when you slip and then you stick,
And the air mixed with the language gets beautifully thick.
The smoke it nearly blinds you and with sulphur you near choke,
You turn to get a drink and find your blooming bottle's broke.

Of course it's not expected that we chaps want much to eat
But now and then we get a chance and it really is a treat.
When you've put your food upon the floor it's enough to raise
    your ire:
Your mate gets absent-minded like and drops it in the fire.

Well, you reach your destination neither happy, blithe, nor gay,
With just enough strength to whistle *End of a perfect day.*
All your hopes are fairly stranded when the turner says, Book off.
Miles away from home you're landed, neither money, 'bacca, scoff.

They send you to a barracks built inside the station yard
Where the engines sing your lullaby and the beds are nice and hard.
Or perhaps it's private diggings, they're another lively hole,
For it's ten to one the blooming fire's gone out to find some coal.

You start the homeward journey and things reach a pretty pass
When you're half-inclined to envy the cattle out at grass,
And you vow you'll chuck your job up, you swear you'll do no
      more.
Reach your home, Come on in nine hours, and the game starts as
      before.

It's a shame they work the drivers till of age they nearly drop,
Why can't they have a pension, like a postman or a slop?
They earn it, they deserve it, and then contented they would be.
Besides, 'twould mean promotion and there'd be a chance for me.

I often wonder if I'll ever get a driver's job
For I'm sick and tired of firing sixty hours for thirty bob.
Perhaps I'll fire until I die and then to heaven I'll go,
Or perhaps I will be firing still for the Old Lad down below.

Some anonymous verses from the columns of the *Railway Gazette,*
which are virtually self-explanatory. Presumably they were written
as a recitation, but they sing well to *Castles in the air* or any similar
tune. Things are better now, both as regards wages and working
conditions, but the hierarchical system referred to in the last two
verses still has its divisive effect.

ON THE OLD ELLENNY

words: Jim Ward

tune: *Bell-bottom trousers*

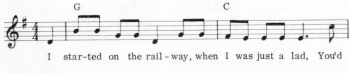

I star-ted on the rail-way, when I was just a lad, You'd

be a-mazed to hear me say the kind of jobs I've had, They

gave me cap and ov - er-coat to keep me dry and warm,

First I had to write and sign an app - lic - at - ion form. A

rail-way-man, a rail - way-man, a rail - way-man you see,

Since the day I star - ted on the old El - len - ny.

I started on the railway when I was just a lad,
You'd be amazed to hear me say the kind of jobs I've had.
They gave me cap and overcoat to keep me dry and warm
First I had to write and sign an application form.
chorus: A railwayman, a railwayman, a railwayman you see,
Since the day I started on the old Ellenny.

When ten years on the railways, then they said to me,
You're going down to Enfield Town. A coalie you will be.
To keep those engines rolling, a job for you we've planned,
Those engines you'll be coaling with a shovel in your hands.

I got transferred to Stratford to keep the carriages clean,
To wash and wipe the windows and give the brass a sheen.
Though I am a carriage-cleaner, I'm very poorly paid,
So I applied to Bishopsgate to get a higher grade.

I've a grade at Bishopsgate, a carman with a mate,
Collecting and delivering sundry kinds of freight.
I almost am contented, I've still one grade to get.
The railways then consented those motors I could set.

Two years on the station spent moving round those loads,
I made an application to go out on the roads.
My application granted, now every day you see
Me driving round those London streets for the Ellenny.

One of the first songs Jim Ward wrote was about his experiences working for the old London and North Eastern Railway or LNE (Ellenny). During the depression 750 London van guards like him were offered jobs 'down the line', sometimes as far away from their families as Leeds. 'For me and them it was a process of transfers from job to job to get back to one's home station,' he recalls. 'I had five transfers back to Bishopsgate.'

TURNTABLE SONG

by Dave Goulder

'Twas half past five on a Wednes-day morn, the dri-ver and his mate___ Came hurt-lin' out o' the lo-co shed in a damn great num-ber eight_____ The fire-man wiped his grea-sy hands as they rolled a-long the track___ To pick up a gal-lon o' wa-ter and a cou-ple o' tubs o'

slack, A cou-ple o' tubs o' slack _____

'Twas half-past five on a Wednesday morn, the driver and his mate
Came hurtlin' out of the loco shed in a damn great number eight.
The fireman wiped his greasy hands as they rolled along the track
To pick up a gallon of water and a couple of tubs of slack,
A couple of tubs of slack.

They waited till the clock was showing a couple of hundred pound,
They took her to the turntable and they quickly turned her round.
But when they went to park her they made their big mistake
For they left her on a gradient and forgot about the brake,
Forgot about the brake.

It happened when the table was only halfway round,
The engine's wheels began to turn with an ominous rumbling sound.
The driver when he saw the thing began to scream and spit
As the mighty engine humped its back and plunged into the pit,
And plunged into the pit.

He went to tell the foreman, he was quaking at the knees.
Saying, Sir you've got an engine parked at forty-five degrees.
The foreman turned a ghastly green and grabbed the telephone.
Then half a bottle of aspirins and he caught the next bus home,
Caught the next bus home.

They fetched the gang from Nottingham and they soon set about
With chains and jacks and dirty words they got the damn thing out.
The fireman lost his shovel, now he's sweeping up the coal,
And I haven't seen the driver since, I think he's on the dole,
Think he's on the dole.

Though now he manages a youth hostel in the Scottish mountains,
Dave Goulder started on the railways at 15, and worked as porter,
fireman, and cleaner. This song is based on a true incident and is
from his collection, *Green All the Way*. He sings it on the LP
Requiem for Steam (Big Ben, BB0004).

DOCTOR BEECHING

tune: *The bonnie lass of Fyvie*

Oh, there came a troop of Irish dragoons
Came marching up through Fyvie, oh,
And the reason that they marched all the way from Marble Arch
There were no railways running up tae Fyvie, oh.

After the '45 was over and done
Geordie said tae Wade, Man alivey, oh,
Grab a pick and grab a spade, don't come back till ye have made
Me a road running all the way tae Fyvie, oh.

So Wade he grabbed a shovel and he built the king a road
It ran through the Borders tae Fyvie, oh.
He built the king a road and it wasnae verra broad
But it speeded the journey up tae Fyvie, oh.

You've all heard of Watt, the celebrated Scot,
Brewing up some coffee after bringin', oh,
As he watched the kettle steam Jimmy Watt began to dream
And invented the very first steam engine, oh.

Soon after came the train, product of a Scottish brain,
And railway lines sprang up to Fyvie, oh,
Aye and many an English chiel made his fortune on the deal
When they built it, the railway line to Fyvie, oh.

But it's different today, for the railways dinna pay
So they called in Doctor Beeching, oh.
He came straight from ICI, in his pukka old school tie,
You should just hear the nonsense he is preaching, oh.

He told Uncle Mac, did this economic quack,
Take all the railway lines from Fyvie, oh,
Take the railway lines away and the bloody things will pay
And the national economy will thrivey, oh.

So now Doctor Dick, don't you play this dirty trick,
If you should value your livey, oh,
Or you'll end up on your back, fastened tae a railway track,
In the path of the last train out of Fyvie, oh.

A pungent comment on the recommendations of an economic
expert called in to make the railways pay, collected by David
Mellors from a Mrs Kirk in Worksop. There is often more sound
common sense in parodies like these—which are very common in
almost all industries—than in thousands of words or reports from
time and motion study experts and efficiency men.

THE REDUNDANT RAILWAYMAN

by Jim Ward

Come listen brother railwaymen, men from every grade,
You'll have to leave the railways now and learn another trade.
They tell us that the railways must be modernised,
We know it's for the profit of private enterprise.

No more across the countryside you'll hear those whistles scream.
They're driving diesel engines now in the place of steam.
Those sundry goods and parcels have gone upon the road,
Those freightline trains all carry now full container loads.

The loco sheds are empty now, their engines gone for scrap,
The train-rides to the countryside no longer on the map,
Each depot, shed and station closed, become disused and die,
Three hundred thousand railwaymen know the reason why.

I started on the railway when I was in my teens,
In those postwar depression years and unemployment scenes.
For forty years my life I've give and now they've said to me,
Reward my faithful service with my redundancy.

THE RAILWAYMAN'S LAMENT

by Jim Ward

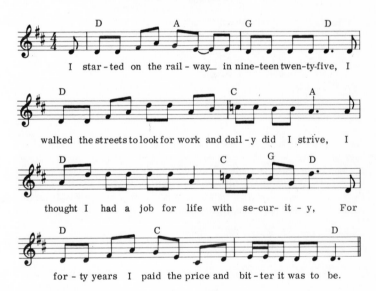

I star-ted on the rail-way— in nine-teen twen-ty-five, I
walked the streets to look for work and dail-y did I strive, I
thought I had a job for life with se-cur-it-y, For
for-ty years I paid the price and bit-ter it was to be.

I started on the railway in nineteen twenty-five.
I walked the streets to look for work and daily did I strive.
I thought I had a job for life with security.
For forty years I paid the price and bitter it was to be.

The first ten years of poverty I find it hard to speak,
To try and keep a family on thirty shillings a week.
They sent me down to Ely and stations down the line,
The railway tried cold-bloodedly to make me the job resign.

81

My wife she went out cleaning to try and make ends meet,
To add it to the little that I sent her every week.
Two long years slowly passed before it was to be,
I returned to Bethnal Green to live with my family.

I battled through six years of war and managed to survive.
I voted for a brave new world in nineteen forty-five.
A name upon the housing list was all they had for me,
Very soon I realised what the future was to be.

I saw a brighter future with railways nationalised,
Then came Doctor Beeching with his plans to modernise.
I heard a conversation upon the telephone,
The closure of our station, my heart was like a stone.

They gave to me a letter, these words to me did say,
You're surplus and redundant with resettlement pay.
They treat me like a unit, dispense with as they please,
They think I can retire and live a life of ease.

They're making me redundant, they're giving me the sack.
When I leave on Friday, I won't be coming back.
To those I leave behind me, to all I wish you well,
You won't be long behind me, the staff of NCL.

When this song was pinned up in the staff canteen at the National
Carriers Ltd (NCL) depot where he worked, it was torn down by a
trade union official who criticised Jim for its bitterness. In
retrospect, Jim feels he may have been right, and would like to
think of a more 'constructive' last verse. But it must be hard to be
constructive when you're on the dole.

THE WEARY
TRADE

THE FOGGY DEW

When I was a bach-el-or,— hair-y and young I fol-lowed the wea - vin' trade,— And all the harm that ev - er I done— I court - ed a serv - ing maid.— I court-ed her— one sum-mer sea-son and part of the win - ter too, ———— And man-y's the time— I rolled her in my arms— all ov - er the fog - gy dew.————

When I was a bachelor, hairy and young, I followed the weavin'
    trade,
And all the harm that ever I done, I courted a serving maid.
I courted her one summer season and part of the winter too,
And many's the time I rolled her in my arms all over the foggy
    dew.

One night as I lay in my bed a-taking my balm of sleep
This pretty fair maid came to me and how bitterly did she weep.
She wept, she cried, she tore her hair, crying, Oh what I shall I do?
For tonight I've resolved to sleep with you for fear of the foggy
    dew.

Now all the first part of the night we both did sport and play
And in the second part of the night she in my arms did lay.
And when broad daylight did appear, she cried, I am undone.
Oh hold your tongue you foolish young girl, for the foggy dew is
    gone.

Supposing that you should have one child it would make you
    laugh and smile.
Supposing that you should have another, it would make you
    think a while.
Supposing that you should have another, another, another one
    too.
It would make you leave off these foolish young tricks and think
    on the foggy dew.

I loved that girl with all my heart, loved her as I loved my life,
And in the second part of that year, I made her my lawful wife.
I never told her of her faults nor never intend to do,
But many's the time as she winks and smiles, I think on the
    foggy dew.

The earliest weavers were itinerant workers, and the reputation for
loose living that they acquired in those days clung to them for
centuries. The weaver's verse in *A ballad of all the trades* in *Pills to
Purge Melancholy* has something of the same flavour:

> *Oh the weaver, the wicked, wicked weaver,*
>
> *That followeth a weary trade,*
>
> *He never shoots his shuttle right*
>
> *But he shoots, but he shoots, but he shoots first at his Maid.*

The widely-known *Foggy dew* popularised first by Carl Sandburg,
who put it in his *Songbag,* and Benjamin Britten, who arranged it
rather archly for Peter Pears to sing, is far from being 'two verses

deep with the night drench of the British Isles' as Sandburg felt; it is a truncated version of a noble and ancient ballad. The full story, as sung by the late Harry Cox, is substantially the same as the broadsheet in the collection of Nottingham University library. Cox also used the variant of the *Ye banks and braes of bonnie Doon* tune (which is probably English, rather than Scottish, in origin, by the way) to which the song is most often sung in England, though when Phil Hammond recorded a somewhat different story for Peter Kennedy in the 1950s, he couldn't remember the tune, and so he sang it to the Sandburg melody. His version also seems to be unique in tradition in retaining the 'I am a bachelor, I live with my son' line in the last verse which so appeals to students and rugby players. On the other hand, the words 'hairy and young' in our version are not traditional, except in the folk clubs; in the broadsheet version it was 'early and young' and Cox actually used to sing 'when I was an old bachelor'. Another folk club amendment, which I haven't adopted, is to have the girl become 'another man's wife' in the last verse. Much print has been spilt over the meaning of the title. In James Reeves' opinion, the words 'foggy dew' may mean 'protracted virginity'. However, dew is often a folk symbol for male semen (as in *Blow away the morning dew*).

There is a recording of Cox singing his version on an album available only from the English Folk Dance and Song Society, 2 Regents Park Road, London NW1, number 1004, though with a repetitive chorus which he never used when I heard him sing it, nor on the now-deleted recording he did for HMV records. Phil Hammond's version, with the Sandburg tune, can be heard on Topic 12T158.

WILL THE WEAVER

Moth - er dear I have got mar - ried
Wish - ing I had long - er tarr-ied
For my wife does curse and swear_
That __ the bree - ches she will wear.

Mother dear I have got married,
Wishing I had longer tarried,
For my wife does curse and swear
That the breeches she will wear.

She does scold and she does riot,
She is costly in her diet.
She does to the tavern go
With Will the weaver, that I know.

Son, dear son, go home and love her,
Never more your mind discover.
Give your woman what's her due
And she'll never trouble you.

Give her food and give her diet,
Give her all things if she's quiet.
If she offers to rebel
Take a stick and bang her well.

Away he went, a neighbour met him,
Told him all things for to fret him,
I'll just tell you who and how
That I saw with your wife just now.

I saw your wife and Will the weaver
Talking free and close together
On the threshold of the door.
I stepped on and saw no more.

Away he went in a great wonder,
Rattling at the door like thunder.
Who is that? the weaver cried.
'Tis my husband, you must hide.

Into the house the husband entered,
Up the chimney Willie ventured,
Searched the house up and down,
But not a soul was to be found.

When he was nearly tired looking
Fortune to the chimney took him.
There he saw a wretched soul
Sitting on the chimney pole.

He put on a rousing fire
For to please his own desire,

Which made the weaver cough and sneeze
Because he sat at little ease.

You never saw a chimney sweeper
Half as black as Will the weaver.
Hands and feet, legs and thighs,
Sent him home with three black eyes.

A very popular song, so popular in fact that it crossed the Atlantic and became a jazz standard that, as *Willie the weeper,* was recorded by Louis Armstrong. There are versions all over the British Isles, but these particular words and tune were collected by Sam Henry from Tyrone Ditches, near Newry.

THE WEAVERS' SONG

When Her - cu - les did use to spin And
Pal - las wrought up - on the loom, Our
trade to flou - rish did be - gin When
con - science went not sell - ing broom.
Then love and friend- ship did a - gree To
keep the bands of am - i - ty.

When Hercules did use to spin,
And Pallas wrought upon the loom,
Our trade to flourish did begin,
When conscience went not selling broom.

chorus: Then love and friendship did agree
         To keep the bands of amity,
         Then love and friendship did agree
         To keep the bands of amity.

When princes' sons kept sheep in field
And queens made cakes of wheaten flour,
The men to lucre did not yield
Which brought good cheer to every bower.

But when the giants huge and high
Did fight with spears like weavers' beams,
Then they in iron beds did lie
And brought poor men to hard extremes.

But while the Greeks besieged Troy
Penelope apace did spin
And weavers wrought with muckle joy
Though little gains were coming in.

Had Helen then sat carding wool,
Whose beauteous face did breed such strife,
She had not been Sir Paris' trull
Nor caused so many to lose their life.

Or had King Priam's wanton son
Been making quills with sweet content,
He had not then his friends undone
When he to Greece a-gadding went.

The cedar trees endure more storms
Than little shrubs that sprout on high.
The weavers live more void of harms
Than princes of great dignity.

The shepherd sitting in the field
Doth tune his pipe with heart's delight.
When princes watch with spear and shield
The poor man soundly sleeps at night.

Yet this by proof is daily tried
For God's good gifts we are ingrate,
And no man through the world so wide
Lives well contented with his state.

This is the song said to have been sung by 200 weavers in the house of John Winscombe, commonly called Jack of Newberry, when Henry VIII visited the factory, as described in *Jack's Pleasant History:* 'Then came His Highness where he saw a hundred looms standing in one room, and two men working in every one, who pleasantly sung in this sort.' If the report is true, it shows that it was not the gathering together of many workers under one roof which was inimical to folk culture, but the fragmentation of the labour process as a result of technological change. Actually, as the Guild system decayed and was replaced by the growth of cottage weaving, there was a brief flowering of communal work before the factory system proper got under way. The *Pleasant History* was written by Thomas Deloney, a silk weaver, who was described by Kemp, in his *Nine Daies Wonder,* as a great balladmaker, so it is possible that he composed it. According to Mr J. Payne Collier, who included it in a collection of 1868, it should be sung to the tune of *Apelles,* but not having been able to trace it, I have set the words instead to the tune of *The Staines Morris,* first seen in an Elizabethan lute book of William Ballet, and included by John Playford in his first edition of *The Dancing Master* in 1650. As William Chappell said of the Maypole song from *Actaeon and Diana* whose words he put to the tune and which are now usually sung to it (and often, wrongly, thought of as traditional), these words seem 'so exactly fitted to the air that, having no guide to the one intended, I have, on conjecture, printed it with this tune.'

THE SPINNING WHEEL

As Jean sat by— her spin-ning wheel A bon-nie lad-die passed her by,— She

kenned him round__ and liked__ him weel,__ Good
faith__ he had__ a bon - ny eye,__ A
weel__ faured lad__ she 'gan__ to feel,__ But
aye__ she turned her spin - ning wheel.

As Jean sat by her spinning wheel
A bonnie laddie passed her by.
She kenned him round and liked him weel,
Good faith he had a bonny eye.
　　A weel-faured lad, she 'gan to feel,
　　But aye she turned her spinning wheel.

He flung his arms around her waist,
The bonnie lassie he embraced.
He kissed her both on cheek and chin
And soon the lassie answered him.
　　To kiss her hand he down did kneel
　　But aye she turned her spinning wheel.

He praised her fingers long and small,
Her golden hair that down did fall.
He said there was no lady fair
That ever could with her compare.
　　The lassie's love he sought to steal
　　But aye she turned her spinning wheel.

Although she seemingly did chide
Yet he would never be denied
But did declare his love the more
Until her heart was wounded sore,
  That she her love could scarce conceal
  But aye she turned her spinning wheel.

As for her yarn, her rock and reel,
And after that her spinning wheel,
He bid her leave them all with speed
And walk with him in yon green glade.
  Her panting heart strange flames did feel
  But aye she turned her spinning wheel.

It's go with me, the laddie said,
It's go with me my bonnie maid.
And to the haycocks I'll take you
And learn ye better work to do.
  Till she forgot her rock and reel
  And left alone her spinning wheel.

Among the pleasant cocks of hay
Then with her bonnie lad she lay,
And to his work he went with skill
And she did learn with right good will.
  Her pleasure I cannot reveal
  But it far surpassed her spinning wheel.

But now you see what's come to pass,
This bonnie youthful yielding lass
Did sigh and bitterly take on
When twenty weeks was come and gone.
  Saying, Now my grief I must reveal.
  Too soon I left my spinning wheel.

I am a damsel now defiled
For here I find myself with child,
And I'm exposed to open shame
For there's no father for the same.
  My virgin treasure he did steal,
  Too soon I left my spinning wheel.

For my young love sad moan I make,
I find him like a painted snake
Whose beauty did my favour win:
He's fair without and false within.

Love's cruel sting I yet do feel,
Too soon I left my spinning wheel.

My plight no memories allow,
For one small dram of pleasure now.
He's gone and yields me no relief,
I bear a hundredweight of grief.
    My wounded heart no tongue can heal,
    Too soon I left my spinning wheel.

This is an amalgamation of two songs. The story of the lass who forgot her spinning wheel was in *Pills to Purge Melancholy* and the sad sequel from the *Roxburgh Ballads* though I found both in John S. Farmer's *Merry Songs and Ballads Prior to the Year AD 1800* which Gershon Legman, that connoisseur of the venereal arts, has described as 'by far the most valuable collection in English of unexpurgated folksongs and ballads and of uncastrated art and folk poetry'. Personally, I found most of Farmer's five volumes pretty poor stuff. Tune from the singing of Betsy Miller of Auchterarder, Ewan MacColl's mother.

MY WINDER

words: Samuel Bamford

tune: *The rose tree in full bearing*

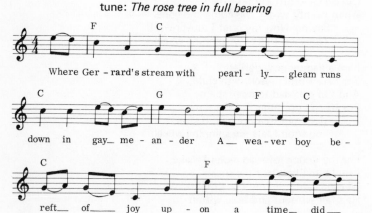

Where Ger - rard's stream with pearl - ly gleam runs down in gay me - an - der A wea - ver boy be - reft of joy up - on a time did

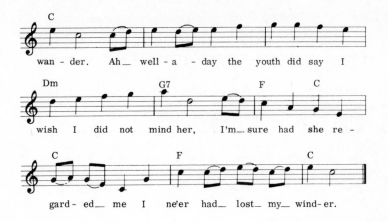

wan - der. Ah__ well - a - day the youth did say I
wish I did not mind her, I'm__ sure had she re -
gard- ed__ me I ne'er had__ lost__ my__ wind- er.

Where Gerrard's stream with pearly gleam runs down in gay ·
    meander,
A weaver boy bereft of joy upon a time did wander.
Ah, well-a-day the youth did say, I wish I did not mind her,
I'm sure had she regarded me, I ne'er had lost my winder.

Her ready hand was white as milk, her fingers finely moulded,
And when she touched a thread of silk, like magic it was folded.
She turned her wheel, she sang her song, and sometimes I have
    joined her.
Oh that one strain would wake again from thee, my lovely winder.

And when the worsted hank she wound, her skill was further
    prov-ed,
No thread uneven there was found, her bobbins never rov-ed.
With sweet content to work she went and never looked behind her
With fretful eye for ills to spy, but now I've lost my winder.

And never would she let me wait when downing on a Friday.
Her wheel went at a merry rate, her person always tidy.
But she is gone and I'm alone, I know not where to find her.
I've sought the hill, the wood and rill, no tidings of my winder.

I've sought her at the dawn of day, I've sought her at the noonin',
I've sought her when the evening grey had brought the hollow
    moon in.
I've called her on the darkest night, with wizard spells to bind her,
And when the stars arose in light I've wandered forth to find her.

Her hair was like the raven's plume and hung in tresses bonnie,
Her cheeks so fair did roses bear that blushed as sweet as any.
With slender waist and carriage chaste, her looks were daily kinder.
I mourn and rave and cannot weave since I have lost my winder.

Bamford was a radical poet whose autobiography was recently reprinted. His song, though couched in somewhat extravagant terms, shows how in the early days one craftsman was very dependent upon the skills of another. With mechanisation this was lost. I sought the tune high and low and was eventually taught it by Carolanne Pegg and Trevor Crozier between them, though since it comes from the repertoire of the Bampton Morris I should have known it. I go to the Oxfordshire village most Whit Mondays.

THE WARK O' THE WEAVERS

by David Shaw

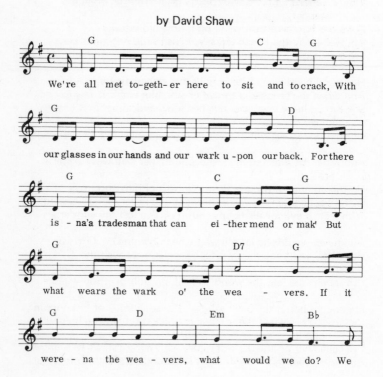

We're all met to-geth-er here to sit and to crack, With our glasses in our hands and our wark u-pon our back. For there is - na'a tradesman that can ei-ther mend or mak' But what wears the wark o' the wea - vers. If it were - na the wea - vers, what would we do? We

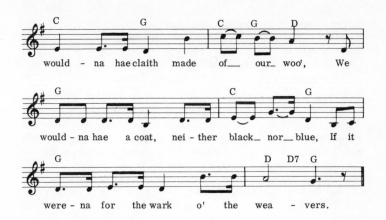

would - na hae claith made of__ our__ woo', We
would - na hae a coat, nei - ther black__ nor__ blue, If it
were - na for the wark o' the wea - vers.

We're all met together here to sit and to crack
With our glasses in our hands and our wark upon our back
For there isna a tradesman that can either mend or mak'
But what wears the wark o' the weavers.
chorus: If it werena the weavers what would we do?
We wouldna hae claith made of our woo',
We wouldna hae a coat, neither black nor blue,
If it werena for the wark o' the weavers.

There's folk independent of other tradesmen's wark,
For women need no barber and dykers need no clerk,
But none of them can do without a coat or a sark,
Which must be the wark o' some weaver.

The ploughmen lads they mock us and crack aye about's,
And say we are thin-faced, bleached-like clouts,
But yet for all their mockery they canna do without's,
No they canna want the wark o' the weavers.

There's smiths and there's wrights and there's masons and a',
There's doctors and dominies and men that live by law,
And our friends in South America, though them we never saw,
And they all need the wark o' the weavers.

Our soldiers and our sailors, o'd, we make them all bold,
For gin they hadna claes, faith, they couldna fecht for cold,
The high and low, the rich and poor, a'body, young and old,
They all need the wark o' the weavers.

So the weaving's a trade that never can fail,
While we aye need a clout to hold another hale,
So let us now be merry ower a beaker of good ale,
And drink to the health of the weavers.

Though the words as sung by Ewan MacColl are these days better known, these lyrics are closer to Shaw's original as printed in Robert Ford's *Vagabond Songs and Ballads of Scotland* in 1899. Ford's notes on the song are worth quoting, if only because he includes fragments of two other songs by Shaw: 'Himself a weaver, the author set his claim beyond dispute to be the accepted laureate of the fidging fraternity, locally, if not generally. In felicitous measures, once and again, he sang the joys and sorrows of the shuttle-driving craft. Thus, in *Tammie Treadlefeet,* who lived in "Shuttle Ha' ", he tells that

> The weaver lads were merry blades
> When Osnaburgs sell'd weel,
> And when the price o' ilka piece
> Did pay a bow o' meal;
> Then fouks got sale for beef and veal,
> For cash was rife wi' everybody,
> And ilka alehouse had the smell
> O' roas'en pies and reekin' toddy.

Now, alas (about the middle of last century), an evil time had fallen on the handloom weaver; but he hopes *'to see the day when trade would tak' a loup'*, and the weavers would again rejoice,

> Wi' fouth o' ale frae cask and pail,
> Or foamin' in a luggit bicker;
> Forbye a dose o' gude thick brose,
> And draps o' gin to haud them siccar.

In *The wark o' the weavers* he claims a dignity for the craft it would be difficult to dispute; and at the same time supplies an ingenious and amusing song. It was originally composed for and sung at the annual meeting of the Forfar Weavers' Friendly Society; but has been sung often since then, and far from the town of Forfar.'

DROYLESDEN WAKES

It's Droyl-sden Wakes, and we're com-ing to town, To
tell you of sum-mat of great— re-nown; And
if this old jade 'll let me be-gin, I'll
show you how hard and how fast I can spin.

CHORUS
So it's three - dy weel three - dy weel
Dan, don, dill, doe, So it's three - dy weel
three- dy weel, Dan, don, dill, doe.

It's Droylesden Wakes and we're coming to town
To tell you of summat of great renown
And if this old jade'll let me begin
I'll show you how hard and how fast I can spin.

chorus: So it's threedyweel, threedyweel,
          Dan, don, dill doe.
          So it's threedyweel, threedyweel,
          Dan, don, dill, doe.

Thou cankered old besom, I cannot endure
Any longer a temper like thine is, I'm sure.
The tow that I spin is five shilling a pound
And that you mun know by my wheel going round.

Thou brags of thyself but I dunno think it's true
For I will uphold thee, thy faults aren't a few,
For when thou hast done, and spun very hard,
Of this I'm well sure, thy work is ill-marred.

Thou saucy old jade, thou'd best hold thy tongue
Or else I must be thumping thee ere it be long.
And if that I do, thou'rt sure for to rue,
For I can have many a one's good as you.

What is it to me who you can have?
I shanno be long ere I'm laid in my grave
And when that I'm dead and have done what I can
You may find one that'll spin as hard as I've done.

Come, come, my dear wife, I'll not have thee rue,
And this I will tell you, and I'll tell you true.
Now if you'll forgive me for what I have said,
I'll do my endeavour to please you instead.

I'm glad for to hear that you will me forgive
And I will do by you as long as I live.
So let us unite and live free of sin
And then we shall have nowt to think on but spin.

So now let's conclude and here endeth our song,
I hope it has pleased this numerous throng,
But if it has missed, you needn't to fear,
We'll do our endeavour to please you next year.

These days a Wakes week usually lasts a fortnight, but when the custom started during the early 19th Century days of the textile industry, it was just a few days off for feasting and dancing, extending gradually to a week. A note in the *Stockport Advertiser* for August 5, 1825, described the enjoyments at Didsbury Wakes as 'chiefly of ass-races for purses of gold, prison-bar playing and grinning through collars for ale, bag-racing for hats, foot-racing for sums of money, maiden plates for ladies under twenty years of age for gown pieces, shawls, etc., treacled-loaf eating for various rewards, wheelbarrow races, the best heats, smoking matches, apple-dumpling eating, bell racing, and balls each evening.' Pruw Edwards has suggested a connection between the Wakes and some pre-Christian pagan custom, especially in view of the association of the word 'wake' with the Celtic custom of merrymaking around the dead, and this song helps to bear this out, for as Lloyd has pointed out, 'the tune is of the primitive sort often used for wassails, May Day songs and other festive ceremonial purposes.' In its present form, however, the song was first noticed about 1814, although before it was sung in Droylesden it had been performed in Woodhouses, near Failsworth. The account of John Higson, a pioneer Lancashire folksong collector, was quoted in John Harland's *Ballads & Songs of Lancashire* (Routledge, 1875): 'The ceremonial issued from Greenside, a hamlet in Droylesden, and consisted of two male equestrians grotesquely habited. One, John, son of Robert Hulme of Greenside, personified a man; the other, James, son of Aaron Etchells of Edge Lane, a woman. They were engaged with spinning wheels, spinning flax in the olden style, and conducting a rustic dialogue in limping verse, after which they collected contributions from spectators. Latterly, a cart was substituted for a saddle, as being a safer position in case they grew tipsy . . . On one occasion "her" husband got so tipsy that he fell off his horse in the yard of Cinderland Hall, and "she" had to extemporise and instruct another to take his part . . .'

A man dressing up as a woman is an ancient folk custom, far older than notions of drag. According to a pamphlet of June 1649, when the local people of Cobham and Walton attacked Gerrard Winstanley and his Diggers on St George's Hill, they put on 'woman's apparell', and during the attack by Luddites in Carwright's mill in April 1812, 'They were nearly all disguised, some having their faces simply blackened and others wearing masks to conceal their features effectually. Many of them were dressed in carters' smock frocks, others had their coats turned inside out, some had put their checked shirts over their clothes, and a few had actually dressed themselves partly in women's apparel,' according to Frank Peel, in *The Risings of the Luddites* (1880). Anyone familiar with ritual clothing will recognise the description, for the Luddite risings were a true folk revolt, such as Britain had not seen since 1381. Gardiner collected a version from a man in Droylesden called Allan Bates and a four-verse version was published in *The Penguin Book of English Folk Song.* It is this which Ewan MacColl sings on Topic 12T104. The meaning of the chorus has never been satisfactorily explained, though it may mean 'thread the wheel'.

THE LINT PULLING

When— I was young and pulled at lint I was hand-some spry and trig—— I al-ways kept in— tem-per with the lass was on my rig—— And if the— pull-ers— chanced to kemp no mat-ter who was late—— I— ay took spe-cial cau-tion that my— lass was— ne-ver beat.——

When I was young and pulled at lint I was handsome, spry, and
        trig.
I always kept in temper with the lass was on my rig,
And if the pullers chanced to kemp, no matter who was late,
I aye took special caution that my lass was never beat.

I once went down by Bushmill's way for they had a boon on there,
It's not for the greed of gear I went but for the spree and tear,
For young ones then, I would have you ken, would fare jump at a
        chance,
And they would work the lee-lang day, at night to get a dance.

The servant girl that was in the house, she was neat, genteel and
        fair,
She had twa bonnie rosy cheeks and a head of curly hair.
Besides she had that winning way that would your favour gain
And I felt my heart a-warming for that maid called Mary Jane.

When we landed on the head rig, the maids they got their choice,
Each to pick her partner from among the men and boys,
And when we started at the foot my heart did jump with glee,
For Mary Jane was on my rig and she had picked on me.

You see I was the stranger there, I had no room to talk,
But them that has the knack can pull as fast as some can walk.
I looked across at Mary Jane and, says I, We've got to pull.
She threw her bonnet down the field and answered back, We will.

I did the sweeping 'cross the rig, she did the breaking in,
And every time we pulled in front I made her take her win,
And though both right and left of us they were pressing us very
        hard,
We were the first two at the head, we had beat them by a yard.

We had scarcely pulled the others out when the bell rang six
        o'clock.
We were all fatigued and wearied, and glad to hear the knock.
My comrade lingering at the gate, it's unto me did say,
If they pull hard tomorrow, Rab, in the rig with you I'll stay.

I helped her fill the creel that night, it was for the morning fire.
I asked her would she like for life with me to come and hire.
Says I, You'll have to work gey hard and your wages won't be big.
She says, We'll pull together, Rab, the way we pulled the rig.

The harvest-time kemp, or reaping contest, is more well-known in
Scotland than in Ireland, and the number of Scotticisms in this

song seems to indicate a Caledonian origin, though the song is now about pulling flax for the linen weavers. The song was collected by Sam Henry from John Elliot, fiddler and singer of Turfahun, Bushmills, and can be heard sung in fine style on Topic 12T209 by Trevor Stewart of Antrim, whose father knew Mr Elliot well.

THE ROVING HACKLER

I am a ro-ving hack-ler lad that loves the sham-rock shore,___ My name is Pat Mc Don-ald and my age is eigh-ty four,___ Be-loved and well re-spec-ted by my neigh-bours one and all___ On St. Pat-rick's Day I loved to stray round Lav-ey and Grouse Hall.___

I am a roving hackler lad that loves the shamrock shore,
My name is Pat McDonald and my age is eighty-four,
Beloved and well respected by my neighbours one and all.
On St Patrick's Day I love to stray round Lavey and Grouse Hall.

When I was young I danced and sung and drank good whiskey too,
In each shebeen shop that sold a drop of the real old mountain dew.
With a poteen still on every hill the peelers had no call
Round sweet Stradone to be well known, round Lavey and Grouse
      Hall.

I rambled round from town to town for hackling was my trade,
None can deny, I think, that I an honest living made.
Where e'er I'd stay by night or day, the youth would always call
To have some crack with Paddy Jack, the hackler from Grouse
      Hall.

I think it strange how times have changed so very much of late.
Coercion now is all the go and peelers on their beat.
To take a glass is now alas the greatest crime of all
Since Balfour placed that hungry beast the sergeant of Grouse Hall.

That busy tool of Castle rule, he travels night and day,
He'll seize a goat tight by the throat for want of better prey.
That nasty skunk, he'll swear you're drunk though you took none
      at all.
There is no peace about the place since he came to Grouse Hall.

'Twas on pretence of this offence he dragged me off to jail,
Alone to dwell in a stone-cold cell my fate for to bewail.
My hoary head on a plank bed, such wrongs for vengeance call.
He'll rue the day he dragged away the hackler from Grouse Hall.

He haunts the League, just like a plague, and shame for to relate,
The priest can't be on Sunday free the Mass to celebrate.
It's there he'll kneel, encased in steel, prepared on duty's call,
For to assail and drag to jail our clergy from Grouse Hall.

Down into hell he'd run pellmell to hunt for poteen there
And won't be loth to swear an oath 'twas found in Killinkere.
He'll search your bed from foot to head, sheets, blankets, tick, and
      all.
Your wife, undressed, must leave the nest for Jemmy of Grouse
      Hall.

He fixed a plan for that poor man who had a handsome wife
To take away without delay her liberty and life.
He'd swear quite plain that he's insane and got no sense at all
As he has done of late with one convenient to Grouse Hall.

His raid on dogs I'm sure it flogs, it's shocking to behold
How he'll pull up a six-months' pup and swear it's a two-year-old.
Outside of hell a parallel can't be found for him at all,
For that vile pimp and devil's imp, the ruler of Grouse Hall.

Thank God the day isn't far away when Home Rule will be seen
And brave Parnell at home will dwell and shine in College Green.
Our policemen will all be then our nation's choice and all,
Old Balfour's pack will get the sack and banished from Grouse Hall.

Let old and young clear up their lungs and sing this little song,
Come join with me and let him see you all resent the wrong.
And while I live I'll always give a prayer for his downfall,
And when I die I don't deny I'll haunt him from Grouse Hall.

The old Irish threat — 'take care, or I'll make a ballad about ye' —
came true in this old song, which must be at least eighty years old.
Balfour was England's Chief Secretary for Ireland from 1886 to
1892, and Parnell fell from grace in 1890. Colm O Lochlainn has
the words of a reply by the police sergeant pilloried in this song,
though since it merely perpetuates the ridicule of the earlier song I
have doubts that the peeler himself wrote it. It reads more like salt
rubbed in the wound by the ardent moonshiner and Home Ruler
who made the first. A hackler used to travel from door to door
fining down flax to get it ready for spinning. The version and
sequel were got by O Lochlainn from Mr John Smith of
Stravicnabo, Ballyjamesduff, Co. Cavan, once a great region for
flax-growing, but no more, alas.

THE WEAVER OF WELLBROOK

by Ben Brierley

You gent - le -men all with your hounds and your parks You may
gam - ble and sport till you dee, But a
qui - et house'nook, a good wife and a book Is
more to the lik - ings of me_____ With my
pick - ers and pins And my well - ers to't shins, My
lin - der - ins, shut - tle and yeald - hook My___
tread - les and sticks_ My weight ropes and bricks, What a
life said the wea - ver of Well - brook.

You gentlemen all with your hounds and your parks
You may gamble and sport till you dee,
But a quiet house nook, a good wife and a book
Is more to the likings of me.

chorus:　With my pickers and pins
　　　　　And my wellers to the shins,
　　　　　My linderins, shuttle and yealdhook,
　　　　　My treadles and sticks,
　　　　　My weight-ropes and bricks,
　　　　　What a life, said the weaver of Wellbrook.

I care not for titles, nor houses, nor land,
Old John's a name fitting for me,
And give me a thatch with a wooden door-latch,
And six feet of ground when I dee.

Some folk like to stuff their old wallets with meat,
Till they're as round and as brawsen as frogs,
But for me I'm content when I've paid down my rent
With enough to keep me up in my clogs.

And there some are too idle to use their own feet
And mun cower and stroddle in th'lone,
But when I'm wheeled or carried it'll be to get buried,
And then Dicky-up with Old John.

You may turn up your noses at me and th'old dame
And thrutch us like dogs agen the wall,
But as long's I can nigger I'll ne'er be a beggar
So I care not a cuss for you all.

Then Margit turn round that old hum-a-drum wheel
And my shuttle shall fly like a brid,
And when I no longer can use hand or finger
They can say, While I could do I did.

This song by a radical weaver poet born in Failsworth, near
Oldham, in 1825, was printed in Harland's *Ballads & Songs of
Lancashire*, and sung to this melody by Harry Boardman on Topic
12T125.

THE HANDLOOM WEAVER AND
THE FACTORY MAID

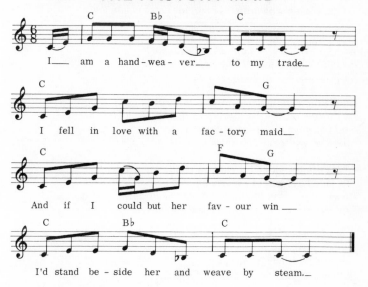

I am a hand-weaver to my trade,
I fell in love with a factory maid,
And if I could but her favour win
I'd stand beside her and weave by steam.

This pretty maid is proud as a queen,
With a handloom weaver she'd never be seen.
So I sit sad at work all day,
This lass she has stolen my heart away.

My father to me scornful said,
How could you fancy a factory maid
When you could have girls fine and gay
And dressed like to the Queen of May?

As for your fine girls, I don't care,
And could I but enjoy my dearest dear,
I'd stand in the factory all the day
And she and I'd keep our shuttles in play.

I went to my love's bedroom door,
Where oftentimes I had been before,
But I could not speak nor yet get in
To the pleasant bed my love laid in.

How can you say it's a pleasant bed
When nowt lies there but a factory maid?
A factory lass although she be,
Blest is the man that enjoys she.

Oh pleasant thoughts came to my mind
As I turned down the sheets so fine,
And I saw her two breasts standing so
Like two white hills all covered with snow.

Where are the girls? I'll tell you plain,
The girls have gone to weave by steam,
And if you'd find them, you must rise at dawn
And trudge to the mill in the early morn.

A weaver lad I'll always be,
If this pretty fair maid will have me,
And if I can't her favour gain
I'll have to go back to my loom again.

This song from the earliest days of industrialism is actually much older, and the story of its ancestry illustrates neatly what is known sometimes as the folk process, by which old songs become adapted to new purposes. In the library at Cecil Sharp House is a broadside printed by Walkden called *The weaver in love* in which the object of his affections is not a factory maid but a serving maid, but the response of his father is equally contemptuous. On the other hand, Frank Kidson collected a song he called *The Yorkshire weaver,* which he printed in 1929, in which the boot is rather on the other foot, the weaver's love being described as *the finest lass in Morley town,/She always walks out in a fine silk gown,/At weaver lad she looks in scorn,/I wish that a weaver I'd ne'er been born.* Either way, it's fascinating to see how the emotional energy of one or other of these old originals has been tapped to vent the craft scorn of the handworker towards the factory-worker, plus the realisation that all things must pass, even this. Lloyd sings this on his *Iron Muse* compilation, Topic 12T86.

THE MAID OF CAMPBELLS MILL

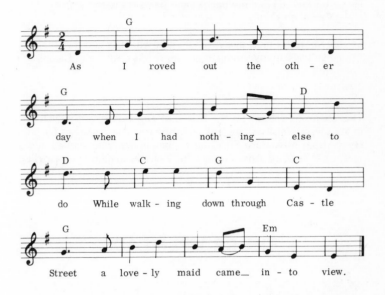

As I roved out the other day when I had nothing else to do
While walking down through Castle Street a lovely maid came into
    view.

She had a nice pink cotton gown bound with a light blue frill.
That moment Cupid stung my heart for the maid of Campbell's
    mill.

Said I, Fair maid, what is your name? Be pleased to let me know.
Do you stray far along this way for along with you I'd like to go?

My name to you, sir, I won't tell but I reside in Carrick Hill.
A man like you, what would you do, with a girl that works in
    Campbell's mill?

Your enchanting looks have won my heart, one look of you is fit
    for to kill.
So come with me no more to roam so early to the spinning mill.

Oh no, kind sir, I'll mind my trade and I would have you under-
    stand
That I'm no equal match for you, a fine well-looking gentleman.

And I gave my hand to a young man whose charms to me my
  bosom fill.
He's a heckler lad and my delight and he works with me in
  Campbell's mill.

So fare ye well, I must away, for the last whistle's said its will.
I must go back to my young man who works with me in Campbell's
  mill.

This charming variant on the theme of *The factory girl* (which see,
in its several versions, ancient and modern) was collected by Sam
Henry from Miss Mary Forsythe at Balnamore, who learned it, she
said, of Miss Mary Ann Young of Liscolman some 50 years earlier.

THE CROPPER LADS

Come crop-per lads of great re-nown Who love to drink good
ale__ that's brown And strike each hau-ghty ty-rant down, With
hat-chet pike and gun. O, the crop-per lads for
me. And gal-lant lads they be. With
lus-ty stroke the shear frames broke, The cropper lads for me.

Come cropper lads of great renown
Who love to drink good ale that's brown
And strike each haughty tyrant down
With hatchet, pike and gun.

chorus:　Oh, the cropper lads for me
　　　　　And gallant lads they be.
　　　　　With lusty stroke the shearframes broke,
　　　　　The cropper lads for me.

What though the specials still advance
And soldiers nightly round us prance.
The cropper lads still lead the dance
With hatchet, pike and gun.

And night by night when all is still
And the moon is hid behind the hill
We forward march to do our will
With hatchet, pike and gun.

Great Enoch still shall lead the van.
Stop him who dare, stop him who can!
Press forward every gallant man
With hatchet, pike and gun.

Croppers was the Yorkshire name for the men who cut the nap off the woven cloth, using 40-pound shears, to give it a smooth finish, though the agitation against the use of gig mills and cropping machines began in Wiltshire in July 1802. It was widely believed that the use of such machinery infringed a law of the time of Edward VI and in 1793 there had actually been a legal case to test the issue, but it never came to trial. 'Great Enoch' was the name of the hammer used in Yorkshire for smashing the shearframes. There is a spirited account of the singing of this 'Ludd ditty' by John Walker of Longroyd Bridge at the Shears inn, Liversedge in February 1812, by Frank Peel in *The Risings of the Luddites*.

FOSTER'S MILL

Come all you croppers stout and bold
Let your faith grow stronger still.
For the cropper lads in the County of York
Have broken the shears at Foster's Mill.

The wind it blew, the sparks they flew,
Which alarmed the town full soon,
And out of bed poor people did creep
And run by the light of the moon.

Around and around we all will stand
And sternly swear we will:
We'll break the shears and windows too
And set fire to the tazzling mill.

Come all you croppers stout and bold
Let your faith grow stronger still.
For the cropper lads in the County of York
Have broken the shears at Foster's Mill.

I have been unable to find a record of the incident which inspired this song, typical of the best of the cropper ballads. As you might expect from men who spent their working days holding the 40-pound hand-shears horizontal to crop the cloth, the croppers were a tough bunch, and as a result of working in an atmosphere filled with flying fluff, they were great men for their ale. Frank Peel tells the tale of some croppers who were sent to hell: ' . . . in the course of time they became so numerous in that particularly warm region, and withal so very, very unruly, that the devil was at his wit's end what to do with them . . . One day, while pondering on his difficult position, a brilliant idea occurred to his Satanic majesty. He knew the fondness of the croppers when on earth for ale, whether good or bad, so he went to the door of the infernal regions and bawled out "Ale! Ale! Ale!" with all his might. The effect was magical. At the joyful sound all the croppers were seized instantaneously with a burning thirst, and they rushed out to a man, helter skelter. No sooner were they all out than Satan slipped quickly in, bringing the door to and locking it after him, shouting through the keyhole to the astonished and deluded croppers outside: "Now curse you, I've got you out and I'll keep you out. I'll take care no more croppers ever come in here!" And that is given as the reason why no more croppers entered the infernal regions.' This song was first published in *Ballads and Songs* magazine.

GRIMSHAW'S FACTORY FIRE

Come all ye coun-try gen-tle-men come lis-ten to my sto-ry It's of a coun-try gall-ant who was cropped in his glo-ry, All

by a new in - ven - tion as all things come by
na - ture, Con - cern - ing looms from Don - cas - ter and
wea. - ving done by wa - ter. Then eh the looms from
Don - cas - ter that late - ly have come down, That they
ne - ver have been carr-ied in - to Man - ches-ter town.

Come all ye country gentlemen, come listen to my story,
It's of a country gallant who was cropped in his glory
All by a new invention as all things come by nature,
Concerning looms from Doncaster and weaving done by water.
      Then eh the looms from Doncaster that lately have come
         down
        That they never have been carried into Manchester town.

For coal to work his factory he sent unto the Duke, sir,
He thought that all the town should be stifled with the smoke, sir.
But the Duke sent him an answer which came so speedily
That the poor should have the coal if the devil took the machinery.
      Then eh the looms from Doncaster that lately have come
         down
        That they never have been carried into Manchester town.

He got all kinds of people to work at his invention,
Both English, Scotch and Irish and more than I could mention.
He kept such order over them, much more than they did choose,
    sir,
They left him land for liberty, please God to spare their shoes, sir.
        Then eh the looms from Doncaster that lately have come
            down
        That they never have been carried into Manchester town.

The floor was over shavings, took fire in the night, sir,
But now he's sick in bed, some say it's with affright, sir.
Perhaps it was an accident, a spark came from the fire,
But they say the handloom weavers have all got their desire.
        Then eh the looms from Doncaster that lately have come
            down
        That they never have been carried into Manchester town.

John Higson collected this song, believed to be part of a longer
ballad from a Manchester broadside printer, 'from five old men,
each of whom well recollects singing at the time of its currency'. It
is reputed to have been composed by one Lucas, an illiterate handloom weaver and crofter, or bleacher, who lived up the Ginnel,
near Chapelhouses, Gorton. Shortly after the Rev. Dr Cartwright,
inventor of the power loom, had tried and failed to run a
mechanised weaving mill near Doncaster, Robert Grimshaw erected
a factory at Knott Mill with room for 30 of the Doncaster looms,
to be driven by steam. But local opponents of power weaving, it
was said, burnt the mill down — though the official verdict was
that shavings left on the floor caught fire accidentally. Whether or
no, Grimshaw didn't proceed with his plans to utilise up to 500
power looms, which weren't re-introduced west of the Pennines for
another 16 years, until 1806. I found this in Harland's *Ballads and
Songs of Lancashire*.

THE HANDLOOM
VERSUS THE POWERLOOM

Come all you cot-ton wea-vers your looms you may pull down, You must get em-ployed in fac-tor-ies in coun-try or in town. For our cot-ton mas-ters have found out a won-der-ful scheme These cal-i-co goods now wove by hand they're going to weave by steam.

Come all you cotton weavers, your looms you may pull down.
You must get employed in factories, in country or in town,
For our cotton masters have found out a wonderful scheme,
These calico goods now wove by hand they're going to weave by
    steam.

In comes the gruff o'erlooker or the master will attend.
It's, You must find another shop or quickly you must mend.
For such work as this will never do, so now I'll tell you plain,
We must have good pincop spinning, or we ne'er can weave by
    steam.

There's sour-makers and dressers and some are making warps,
These poor pincop spinners they must mind their flats and
    sharps.
For if an end slips under, as sometimes perchance it may,
They'll daub you down in black and white, and you've a shilling
    to pay.

In comes the surly winder, her cops they are all marred,
They are all snarls and soft bad ends, for I've roved off many a yard.
I'm sure I'll tell the master or the joss when he comes in,
They'll daub you down and you must pay, so the money comes
    rolling in.

The weavers' turn will next come on, for they must not escape,
To enlarge the master's fortunes they are fined in every shape,
For thin places, or bad edges, a go, or else a float,
They'll daub you down and you must pay threepence, or else a
    groat.

If you go into a loom-shop, where there's three or four pair of
    looms,
They are all standing empty, encumbrances of the rooms,
And if you ask the reason why, the old mother will tell you plain,
My daughters have forsaken them and gone to weave by steam.

So come all you cotton-weavers, you must rise up very soon,
For you must work in factories from morning, night and noon.
You mustn't walk in your garden for two or three hours a day,
For you must stand at their command and keep your shuttles in
    play.

There are phrases in common between this anti-factory song and
The handloom-weaver and the factory maid, so possibly it was

once sung to the same tune, though for variety's sake it is set here to the melody Harry Boardman used when he sang it on Topic 12T125. The words are from Harland's *Ballads and Songs of Lancashire* which credits them to one John Grimshaw, better known as 'Common', of Gorton, near Manchester. The theme of greedy bosses fining their workers for faults they had not caused is a common one, and not confined to the weaving trade, either.

THE PRIDE OF THE SPRINGFIELD ROW

I took my love___ for a walk in the mer - ry month of May,___ The birds were sing - ing sweet - ly as we went a - long our way___ She said she loved me dear - ly and to me she would be true,___ If you will stay with me my love, sure I will stay with

I took my love for a walk in the merry month of May,
The birds were singing sweetly as we went along our way.
She said she loved me dearly and to me she would be true,
If you will stay with me my love, sure I will stay with you.

chorus: We strolled along the down, the birds sang loud and gay,
It was there I met my little brunette and she stole my
heart away.
Her cheeks they were like roses and her skin as white as
snow.
She was the darling of my heart and the pride of the
Springfield Row.

Now we'll be getting married for she has named the day,
And happy we'll be together as we go along our way.

We'll have a tidy little house and a garden for to till
And we'll bring our children up like us to work in the cotton
    mill.

Now I'll bid yez all good evening for now I must away,
I'm off to see her parents and to hear what they will say.
She says, They'll treat you kindly and the glasses they will fill
And they'll drink a toast to the bride and groom that work in the
    cotton mill.

Verily the practitioners of the roving trade had settled down by the
time this song was made, probably in the Nineteenth Century. It
comes from the repertoire of the McPeake family, but I heard it
sung by the Irish Country Four on Topic 12TS209, with Jess
Harpur singing the verses. Springfield Road is a street in Belfast.

THE DOFFING MISTRESS

Oh do you know her, or do you not, This
new doff-ing mis-tress we have got? Els - ie
Thom - son it is her name, And she
helps her doff - ers on ev - 'ry frame,
Fol - de - ri - fol - rah, fol - de - ri - fol - ree.

Oh do you know her, or do you not,
This new doffing mistress we have got?
Elsie Thomson it is her name
And she helps her doffers on every frame.
      Fol-de-ri fol rah, fol-de-ri fol ree.

On Monday morning when she comes in,
She hangs her coat on the highest pin,
Turns around just to greet her friends,
Crying, Hi, ye doffers, tie up your ends!
      Fol-de-ri fol rah, fol-de-ri fol ree.

Sometimes the boss he looks in the door,
Tie your ends up doffers, he will roar.
Tie your ends up we surely do,
For Elsie Thomson but not for you.
      Fol-de-ri fol rah, fol-de-ri fol ree.

Oh do you know her, or do you not,
This new doffing mistress we have got?
Elsie Thomson it is her name
And she helps her doffers on every frame.
      Fol-de-ri fol rah, fol-de-ri fol ree.

A song from the flax-spinning mills of Northern Ireland, though I heard it first sung by that fine Scottish lass, Ray Fisher. A doffer takes the full bobbins off the spinning machines. The song illustrates the way community loyalty — in this case, the inter-community of the spinning shed — took precedence over the boss-worker relationship. The line about hanging her coat on the highest pin also illustrates the hazards of industrial work, for most spinners were crook-backed as a result of their work. Similarly, long before science discovered vaccination, folk observation had revealed the fact that milking girls seemed to be immune from smallpox in the lines: *Where are you going to, my pretty fair maid?/I'm going a milking sir, she said.* Ray can be heard singing this on Topic 12T86.

THE SPINNER'S WEDDING

The gaffer's looking worried for the flatts are in a steer,
Jessie Brodie's getting married and the morrow she'll no be here.
chorus: Hurrah, hurroo a daddy-oh, hurrah hurroo a daddy-oh,
      Hurrah, hurroo a daddy-oh,
      Jessie's getting married, oh.

The helper and the piecer they went doon the toon last nicht
To buy a wee bit present just to make her hame look bricht.

They bought a chiny tea-set, aye, and a chanty full of salt,
A bonnie coloured carpet, a kettle and a pot.

The spinners they're all singing, the shifters dancing too,
The gaffer's standing watching but there's nothing he can do.

Here's best wishes to ye, lassie, standing at your spinning frame,
May ye aye hae full and plenty in your wee bit hame.

The independence displayed by industrial workers on certain,
specified occasions carries on the old traditions of the Lord of
Misrule as is shown by this song from the Dundee spinning mills. It
can be heard, beautifully sung by Ray Fisher with the equally
lovely voice of Annie Briggs joining in the chorus, on Topic 12T86.

THE POOR COTTON WEAVER

tune: *John of Greenfield*

I'm a poor cot-ton wea-ver as
ma-ny a one knows. I've nowt to eat i' the
house and I've worn out my clothes. You'd

hard - ly give six - pence for all I've got on, My— clogs they are burs - ten and sto - ckings I've none. You'd— think it were hard to— be sent to the ward For to clam and do best that you can.___

I'm a poor cotton weaver as many a one knows,
I've nowt to eat i'the house and I've worn out my clothes.
You'd hardly give sixpence for all I've got on,
My clogs they are bursten and stockings I've none.
    You'd think it were hard to be sent to the ward
    For to clam and do best that you can.

Our cotton masters kept telling me long
We should have better times if I'd but held my tongue.
But I've held my tongue till I can hardly draw breath
And I think in my heart they mean to clem me to death.
    I know they live well by the sweat of our brow
    And dropping our wage every day.

I tarried six weeks, thought each day was the last.
I shifted and chifted till now I'm quite fast.
I lived upon nettles while nettles was good
And Waterloo porridge was t'best of my food.
    I'm telling you true I can find folk enow
    That are living no better than me.

Old Bill o'Dans sent bailiffs one day
For a shop-score I owed him which I could not pay.
But he was too late, for old Bill o'Bent
Had sent tit and cart and ta'en goods for the rent.
      We'd nowt but a stoo' that was seats for two
      And on it cowered Margit and me.

The bailiffs looked round as sly as a mouse
When they saw all things was ta'en out of the house.
Says one to the other, All's gone, thou may see.
Said I, Never fret lads, you're welcome to me.
      They made no more ado but nipped up to th'old stoo'
      And we both went whack upon th'flags.

I got hold of Margit for hoo're stricken sick.
Hoo said hoo ne'er had such a bang sin' hoor wick.
The bailiffs scoured off with th'old stoo' on their back,
They wouldn't have cared had they broken our necks.
      They's mad at old Bent, he'd ta'en goods for rent,
      They was ready to flee us alive.

I said to our Margit as we lay on the floor,
We ne'er shall be lower in this world I'm sure.
But if we alter I'm sure we mun mend
For I think in my heart we are both at far end,
      For meat we have none nor looms to weave on,
      Egad they're as good lost as found.

Then I geet up my piece and took it 'em back,
I scarcely dare speak, master looked so black.
He said, You were o'er-paid the last time you come,
I said, If I was 'twere for weaving 'bout loom.
      In the mind as I'm in, I'll ne'er pick o'er again
      For I've woven myself to th'far end.

Then I come out of th'house and left him to chew that.
When I thought at it again I was vexed till I swat
To think I mun work to keep him and all the set
All the days of my life, and still be in their debt.
      So I'll give over trade and work with a spade
      Or go and break stones upon the road.

Our Margit declared if hoo'd clothes to put on
Hoo'd go up to London to see the great man
And if things were not altered when there hoo had been
Hoo swears hoo would fight with blood up to the een.

Hoo's nowt against th'king but hoo likes a fair thing
And hoo says hoo can tell when hoo can hurt.

The story of the origins of the *John of Greenfield* saga, of which this is one of the most famous instalments, was told by me in *The Cruel Wars.* Suffice it to say that the tune and characters appeared in a whole host of printed broadsides in Napoleonic times, though they were still being written and printed when the French had become our allies against the Russians. I found ten different Greenfield ballads in Cecil Sharp's collection of broadsides, including this one, printed by Wheeler of Whittle Street, Manchester. It is very similar to the words as sung by A.L. Lloyd on Topic 12T86. Ewan MacColl collected a rather different version, which he calls *The four-loom weaver* from Becket Whitehead of Delph, near Oldham, with a noble tune which is, however, rather untypical of the north-west. The title also marks it as of a later date, since multi-loom working was introduced long after the hardships of the early Nineteenth Century.

ALL WISH THE WAR WAS OVER

tune: *The nutting girl*

Since Ad - am's days such times as these Were
nev - er known be - fore, It stuns the old - est
with a - maze, All wish the war was o'er, There's
In - dian wars and Cri - mean wars Not soon to be for-

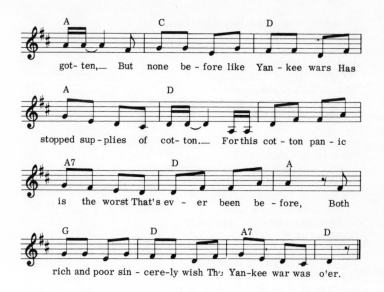

got-ten,— But none be-fore like Yan-kee wars Has stopped sup-plies of cot-ton.— For this cot-ton pan-ic is the worst That's ev-er been be-fore, Both rich and poor sin-cere-ly wish The Yan-kee war was o'er.

Since Adam's days such times as these
Were never known before.
It stuns the oldest with amaze,
All wish the war was o'er.
There's Indian wars and Crimean wars,
Not soon to be forgotten,
But none before like Yankee wars
Has stopped supplies of cotton.
chorus: For this cotton panic is the worst
That's ever been before.
Both rich and poor sincerely wish
The Yankee war was o'er.

There's no mistaken the times are bad,
And still are getting worse.
There's very little to be had
And empty is our purse.
From morning until night
We are sighing all the day,
And saying will these hard times
Never go away?

129

We are waiting till this war shall cease,
And cotton comes again,
When we can go to work in peace
And toil like honest men.
But then the war is raging still
And winter's drawing near.
The piercing cold and wind so shrill
Will very soon be here.

What prospect have the labouring poor
But poverty untold?
There's hundreds beg from door to door,
Both young as well as old.
'Tis hard for honest English pride
So low to be brought down,
While some with plenty turn aside
And treat us with a frown.

But still there's plenty in the land,
There's riches vast in store,
But none that we can now command,
For nothing have the poor.
But still there's some who feel at heart
For all our suffering need
And willingly their aid impart
With charity indeed.

Our trying situation
Most keenly do we feel.
Such long and hard starvation
Would pierce a heart of steel.
But while a helping hand we meet
We'll try to jog along.
Our bitter things may soon be sweet:
The war makes all things wrong.

A song from the cotton famine during the American Civil War,
found on a contemporary broadside. The tune, sometimes known
as *A-nutting we shall go,* is very closely related to another tune
very popular among the cotton radicals, *A-hunting we shall go,*
used for the song, *With Henry Hunt we'll go,* about Peterloo, and
also a number of songs about Wellington, pro and con.

THE HANDLOOM WEAVER'S LAMENT

tune: *The battle of Waterloo*

You gent - le - men and trades - men that ride a - bout at will, Look down on these poor peo - ple it's en - ough to make you chill, Look down on these poor peo - ple as you ride up and down, I think there is a God a - bove will bring your pride quite down. You tyr - ants of England your race may soon be run, You may be brought un - to ac - count for what you've sore - ly done.

You gentlemen and tradesmen that ride about at will,
Look down on these poor people, it's enough to make you chill.
Look down on these poor people, as you ride up and down,
I think there is a God above will bring your pride quite down.

chorus: You tyrants of England, your race may soon be run,
          You may be brought unto account for what you've
            sorely done.

You pull down our wages shamefully to tell,
You go into the markets and say you cannot sell,
And when that we do ask you when these bad times will mend
You quickly give an answer, When the wars are at an end.

When we look on our poor children, it grieves our hearts full sore,
Their clothing it is worn to rags while we can get no more.
With little in their bellies, they to their work must go,
Whilst yours do dress as manky as monkeys in a show.

You go to church on Sundays, I'm sure it's nought but pride,
There can be no religion where humanity's thrown aside.
If there be a place in heaven as there is in the Exchange,
Our poor lost souls must not come near there, like lost sheep they
        must range.

With the choicest of strong dainties your tables overspread,
With good ale and strong brandy, to make your faces red.
You called a set of visitors, it is your whole delight,
And you lay your heads together to make our faces white.

You say that Bonyparty, he's been the spoil of all,
And that we have got reason to pray for his downfall.
Now Bonyparty's dead and gone, and it is plainly shown
That we have bigger tyrants in Bonys of our own.

And now lads for to conclude it's time to make an end,
Let's see if we can form a plan that these bad times may mend.
Then give us our old prices as we have had before,
And we can live in happiness and rub off the old score.

A song collected by John Higson from Common John Grimshaw,
and sung to the tune that was also taken by the radical songmakers
after the massacre of Peterloo for the anti-Wellington song, *With
Henry Hunt we'll go.*

POVERTY KNOCK

Pov-er-ty, pov-er-ty knock, my loom is a-say-ing all day. Pov-er-ty, pov-er-ty knock, gaf-fer's too skin-ny to pay. Pov-er-ty, pov-er-ty, knock, keep-ing one eye on the clock. I know I can gut-tle when I hear my shut-tle Go, pov-er-ty, pov-er-ty knock.

Up ev-ery morning at five, I won-der that we keep a-live, Tir-ed and yaw-ning in the cold

morn-ing, It's back to the drear-y old drive.

chorus: Poverty poverty knock, my loom is a-saying all day.
Poverty poverty knock, gaffer's too skinny to pay.
Poverty poverty knock, keeping one eye on the clock.
I know I can guttle when I hear my shuttle
Go poverty poverty knock.

Up every morning at five, I wonder that we keep alive,
Tired and yawning in the cold morning,
It's back to the dreary old drive.

Oh dear, we're going to be late, gaffer is stood at the gate.
We're out of pocket, our wages they're docket,
We'll have to buy grub on the slate.

And when our wages they'll bring, we're often short of a string.
While we are fratching with gaffer for snatching,
We know to his brass he will cling.

We've got to wet our own yarn, by dipping it into the tarn.
It's wet and soggy and makes us feel groggy
And there's mice in that dirty old barn.

Oh dear, my poor head it sings, I should have woven three strings.
But threads are breaking and my back is aching,
Oh dear, I wish I had wings.

Sometimes a shuttle flies out and gives some poor woman a clout.
There she lies bleeding but nobody's heeding,
Who's going to carry her out?

Tuner should tackle my loom but he'd rather sit on his bum.
He's far too busy a-courting our Lizzie
And I cannot get him to come.

Lizzie is so easy led, I think that he takes her to bed.
She always was skinny, now look at her pinny,
It's just about time they was wed.

Tony Green of Leeds University's unique Institute of Folk Life Studies collected this onomatopoeic song from Mr Tom Daniel of Batley who said he learnt it at the beginning of the century at his first mill on leaving school. The words 'poverty knock' in the chorus and title are supposed to reproduce the sound of the beams on the old Dobbie loom.

THE SHURAT WEAVER

words: Samuel Laycock
tune: *Rory O'More*

Con-found it, I ne'er were so wo-ven a-fore. My
back's well-y brok-en, my fin-gers are sore. I've been
star-in' and root-in' a-mong this Shu-rat Till I'm
ve-ry near get-ting as blind as a bat. Ev-'ry
time I go in with my cuts to old Joe He
gives me a cur-sin' and bates me and all. I've a

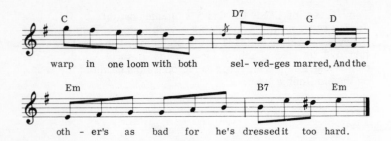

warp in one loom with both sel-ved-ges marred, And the

oth-er's as bad for he's dressed it too hard.

Confound it, I ne'er were so woven afore.
My back's welly broken, my fingers are sore.
I've been starin' and rootin' among this Shurat
Till I'm very near gettin' as blind as a bat.
    Every time I go in with my cuts to old Joe
    He gives me a cursin' and bates me and all.
    I've a warp in one loom with both selvedges marred,
    And the other's as bad for he's dressed it too hard.

I wish I were far enough off, out of th'road,
For of weavin' this rubbish I'm gettin' reet stowed.
I've nowt in this world to lie down on but straw
For I've only eight shillin' this fortnight to draw.
    Now I haven't my family under my hat,
    I've a wife and six children to keep out of that.
    So I'm rather among it, at present, you see,
    If ever a fellow were puzzled, it's me.

If one turns out to steal, folk'll call me a thief
And I canno' put th'cheek on to ax for relief.
As I said in our house t'other neet to my wife,
I never did owt of this sort in my life.
    One doesn't like everyone to know how they are
    But we'n suffered so long through this 'Merica war,
    That there's lots of factory folk gettin' to far end
    And they'll soon be knocked o'er if these times doesn't mend.

Oh dear, if yond Yankees could only just see
How they're clammin' and starvin' poor weavers like me,
I think they'd soon settle their bother and strive
To send us some cotton, to keep us alive.
    There's thousands of folk just in the best of their days
    With traces of want plainly seen in their face,
    And a future afore them as dreary and dark,
    For when th'cotton gets done we shall all be wi'out wark.

We'n been patient and quiet as long as we con,
Th'bits of things we had by us are welly all gone.
I've been tramping so long my old shoon are worn out
And my holiday clothes are all on 'em up the spout.
  It were nobbut last Monday I sold a good bed,
  Nay, very near gave it, to get us some bread.
  Afore these bad times come I used to be fat
  But now, bless your life, I'm as thin as a lath.

Many a time in my life I've seen things looking fou',
But never as awkward as what they are now.
If there isn't some help for us factory folk soon
I'm sure we shall all be knocked reet out of tune.
  Come, give us a lift, you that have owt to give,
  And help your poor brothers and sisters to live.
  Be kind and be tender to th'needy and poor
  And we'll promise when th'times mend we'll ax you no
    more.

During the American Civil War the Northern blockade of the Southern cotton ports caused much hardship in Lancashire (see *All wish the war was over*) and forced the weavers to seek elsewhere for their cotton. The stuff that came from the East India Company's Shurat depot near Bombay was particularly bad, so bad in fact that the very term 'Shurat' became applied (like another weaving term, 'shoddy') to anything inferior. There's a record of a Lancs brewer sueing a customer for slandering his brew as 'Shurat beer'. To add injury to the insult of having to weave such rubbish, the workers were often 'bated' or fined for bad workmanship that was none of their fault, and their pockets suffered still more. Nevertheless, most cotton weavers were strong in support of the Northern cause, for they had a strong radical tradition extending back to before the factory system. This song was written by Samuel Laycock, a weaver who become librarian of Stalybridge Mechanics' Institute and built himself a deservedly high reputation throughout the north-west as a dialect poet on the basis of his songs and poems printed on ha'penny sheets. Harry Boardman has popularised this song, though to a different tune of his own devising.

SURAT WARPS

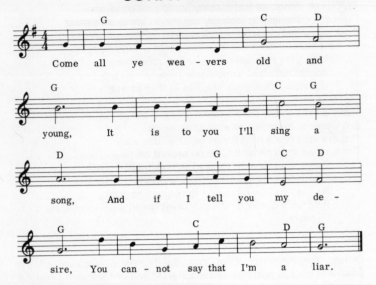

Come all ye weavers old and young,
It is to you I'll sing a song,
And if I tell you my desire,
You cannot say that I'm a liar.

I wish I had these warpers and
All sallywinders in a band.
I'd make the whole of them to groan,
I'd cudgel every one their bones.

Their knots when they come up to th'yealds,
They sweep them just like bumshells.
They fly across the shed and break,
They sweep down all within their reyk.

I look at th'yealds and there they stick,
I ne'er seed the like sin' I were wick.
What pity could befall a heart
To think about these hard-sized warps.

'Twill make the Master for to stare
To see his cloth so rough and bare.
He turns it over, every plait,
He turns it up and cracks to bate.

So I mun at his table stand
And dare not stir one foot or hand
To see him rip the piece to rags
Or give me the eternal bag.

Thus weavers are brought in for all,
Both cops and bobbins, grease and all,
Both warpers, winders, spinners too,
For all their faults they are put through.

Ah, what a spot for weavers here.
It makes me shiver and so queer,
Yet for all this I cannot help
It makes me fit to hang myself.

The gentleman who contributed this song from Bacup, Lancs, to the June 3, 1865 edition of *Notes and Queries* said merely that the weavers who composed it 'sing it to one of their easy-going psalm tunes with much gusto', not specifying which one they used. I have chosen a fairly well-known tune, but you may with equal justification sing any other. For more about the problems of weaving Surat, or Shurat, see Samuel Laycock's *The Shurat weaver.*

COLLIER LADS FOR EVERMORE

SIX JOLLY MINERS

It's of six jolly miners, six miners you shall hear, And we have been a-mining for many a long year, And we've travelled old England, Ireland and Scotland all round, Just digging up the treasure my boys that lies beneath the ground.

It's of six jolly miners, six miners you shall hear,
And we have been a-mining for many a long year,
And we've travelled old England, Ireland and Scotland all round,
Just digging up the treasure, my boys, that lies beneath the ground.

There's one that comes from Cornwall and two from Derby town,
The other three from Williamsbridge, young lads of high renown.
And all of our delight is to split these rocks in twain,
And it's all for the treasure, my boys, as we do undermine.

The huntsman's delight is in blowing of his horn,
And the farmer's delight is in mowing of his corn,
But all of our delight is to split those rocks in twain,
And it's all for the treasure, my boys, as we do undermine.

You should see us miner lads as we walk down the street,
All dressed up in our very best, so gentle and so neat,
With eyes as white as ivory and eyes as black as sloes,
You can easy tell a miner lad everywhere he goes.

My love has knit a grovet as fancy as can be,
The colours she has put in it will fairly take your e'e.
My marrows all come up to me and say, Where got ye that?
I got it from my doggie moll and what d'you think of that?

'Twas down by a crystal river stream I heard a fair maid say,
Oh haven't you seen my miner and has he been this way?
Oh haven't you seen my miner, so sweetly sang she,
For of all the trades in England the miner is for me.

I'll build my love a castle, a castle of renown,
No king nor duke nor earl shall pull my castle down.
The king loves the queen and the emperor does the same
And I love my miner lad and who can me blame?

Sometimes we have money, boys, and sometimes none at all,
But we have got good credit, my boys, when we do have to call.
We fill our glasses merrily and drink the healths around,
And good luck to all jolly miners a-working underground.

A very widespread song which may have originated in Scotland,
but is particularly popular in the rural south of England, possibly
as a result of a broadside version. It is also found in the USA and
Nova Scotia. The tune was found by Gardiner in Hampshire.

THE COLLIER LADDIE

I've travelled east and I've travelled west,
And I hae been to Kirkcaldy,
But the bonniest lass that e'er I spied,
She was following her collier laddie.

She'd silver slippers on her feet,
Her body neat and handsome,
And sky-blue ribbons in her hair
Where gold and jewels were glancing.

Oh, where live ye, my bonnie lass,
And tell me what they call ye?
Bonnie Jean Gordon is my name
And I'm following my collier laddie.

How could you fancy one that's black
And you so fine and gowdie?
Oh fancy one of higher degree
Than to follow your collier laddie.

Oh see you not yon high, high hills
That the sun shines on so brawly?
They all are mine and they shall be thine
Gin you leave your collier laddie.

And you will busk in gay attire,
Well buskit up so gowdie,
And maids to wait on every hand
Gin you leave your collier laddie.

Though you had all the sun shines on
And the earth conceals so lowly,
I would turn my back on you and it all
And embrace my collier laddie.

But he has gone to her father dear,
To her father dear so brawly,
Saying, You'll make your daughter wed with me
And forsake her collier laddie.

How could she fancy one that's black
And her so fine and gowdie?
I'll raise her up to a higher degree
Than to follow a collier laddie.

Her father dear then vowed and sware,
Though he be black he's bonnie.
She's more delight in him, I fear,
Than you with all your money.

I'll give her lands, I'll give her rents,
And I'll make her a lady.
I'll raise her up to a higher degree
Than to follow her collier laddie.

Then he has to his daughter gone,
To his daughter gone so brawly,
Saying, You'll gang with this gentleman
And forsake your collier laddie.

He'll give you lands, he'll give you rents,
And he'll make you a lady.
He'll raise you up to a higher degree
Than to follow your collier laddie.

I winna have his lands and I winna have his rents
And I winna be his lady,
But I'll turn my back on him and it all
And embrace my collier laddie.

It's I can win my five pennies a day,
And spend't at night full brawly,
And I'll make my bed in a collier's neuk
And lie down with my collier laddie.

Now twenty years have come and gone,
Twenty years so brawly,
The same silly old lord came a-begging his bread
From Jean and her collier laddie.

Oh, where's all the lands, and where's all the rents
That was to make me a lady?
I've got gold and gear enough for twa
And I'm aye with my collier laddie.

Now she has to her father gone,
To her father gone so brawly,
Saying, What you'd give to your braw gentleman
You'll give to my collier laddie.

He's counted down five hundred pounds,
Five hundred pounds so brawly,
Saying, Take you that, my daughter Jean,
And give it to your collier laddie.

Oh, love for love is the bargain for me,
Though the wee cot-house should hold me,
And the world's before me to win my bread
And to share with my collier laddie.

Ewan MacColl sang this on one of the first LPs of British folksong
ever produced, accompanied by Brian Daly's guitar, if I remember
rightly. Since then I have got to know Hamish Henderson's rather
longer version, in which the presumptuous lord gets his come-
uppance, and the two have become amalgamated. There was a
version, closer to Henderson's, in Ord's *Bothy Songs and Ballads*.

WALKER SHORE AND BYKER HILL

tune: *Up she goes*

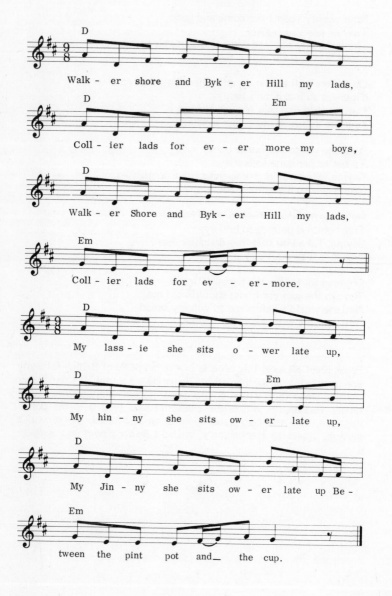

Walk - er shore and Byk - er Hill my lads,

Coll - ier lads for ev - er more my boys,

Walk - er Shore and Byk - er Hill my lads,

Coll - ier lads for ev - er - more.

My lass - ie she sits o - wer late up,

My hin - ny she sits ow - er late up,

My Jin - ny she sits ow - er late up Be -

tween the pint pot and the cup.

chorus: Walker shore and Byker Hill my lads,
          Collier lads for ever more my boys,
          Walker shore and Byker Hill my lads,
          Collier lads for ever more.

My lassie she sits ower late up,
My hinny she sits ower late up,
My Jinny she sits ower late up
Between the pint pot and the cup.

It's down the pits we'll go my laddies,
It's down the pits we'll go my marrows,
We'll try our will and use our skill
To cut them ridges down below.

My Jinny she is never near,
My hinny she is never near,
And when I call out, Where's my supper,
She orders up another pint of beer.

When first I came into the dirt
I had no trousers nor pit shirt,
But now I've getten two or three.
Walker pit's done well for me.

Hey lassie come home to your little baby,
Hey hinny come home to your little baby,
Hey Jinny come home to your little baby,
With a pint of beer all under your arm.

The poor coal cutter gets two shillings,
The deputy gets half a crown,
The overman gets five and sixpence, lads,
Just for riding up and down.

Geordie Johnson had a pig
And he hit it with a shovel and it danced a jig,
All the way to Byker Hill
We danced the *Elsie Marley*.

People who think that 'odd' tempi like 5/4, 9/8 and 7/16 are the invention of modern musicians like Dave Brubeck and Don Ellis, beyond the comprehension of simple folks, should have seen the colliers of Tyneside not only singing but actually *dancing* in 9/8. In fact, even many songs apparently in common time have a much more complex rhythmic construction if one studies them in the mouth of the traditional singer, rather than from the printed page.

BYKER HILL AND WALKER SHORE

If I had another penny I would have another gill,
I would make the piper play *The bonnie lads of Byker Hill.*

chorus: Byker Hill and Walker shore,
　　　　Collier lads for ever more,
　　　　Byker Hill and Walker shore,
　　　　Collier lads for ever more.

The pitman and the keelman trim,
They drink bumble made from gin,
Then to dance they do begin
To the tune of *Elsie Marley.*

When first I went down to the pit
I had no trousers nor no pit shirt.
Now I've gotten two or three,
Byker pit's done well by me.

Geordie Johnson had a pig,
He hit it with a shovel and it danced a jig,
All the way to Walker shore,
To the tune of *Elsie Marley.*

Obviously, there are some floating verses which could migrate from the previous song to this one, and vice versa. The old Young Tradition used to sing this at the end of every performance, and a right rousing sound it was. You can still hear them at it, however, through the magic of electronics on Transatlantic TRA SAM 13.

THE COLLIERS RANT

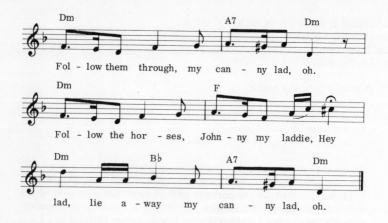

Fol - low them through, my can - ny lad, oh.

Fol - low the hor - ses, John - ny my laddie, Hey

lad, lie a - way my can - ny lad, oh.

As me and my marrow was gannin' to wark
We met with the devil, it was in the dark.
I up with my pick, it being in the neet,
And knocked off his horns, likewise his club feet.
chorus: Follow the horses, Johnny my laddie,
       Follow them through, my canny lad, oh.
       Follow the horses, Johnny my laddie,
       Hey lad, lie away, my canny lad, oh.

As me and my marrow was putting the tram,
The lowe it went out and my marrow went wrang.
You would have laughed had you seen the gam,
Old Nick got my marrow, but I got the tram.

Oh marrow, oh marrow, now what d'you think?
I've broken my bottle and spilt all my drink.
I've lost all my shin-splints among the great stones,
Draw me to the shaft, it's time to gan home.

Oh marrow, oh marrow, where hast thou been?
Driving the drift frae the low seam,
Driving the drift frae the low seam,
Hold up the lowe, lad, de'il stop out thy een.

Oh marrow, oh marrow, this is wor pay week,
We'll get penny loaves and drink to our beek,
And we'll fill up our bumper and round it shall go,
Follow the horses, Johnny lad, oh.

There is my horse and there is my tram,
Two horns full of grease will make her to gan,
There is my hoggers, likewise my half shoon,
And smash my heart, marrow, my putting's all done.

This is the song that was performed with such enthusiasm on vesting day for Britain's newly-nationalised coal industry; how soon the human potential of those early post-war years was dissipated into bureaucracy and cynicism! The song is old, dating to the 18th Century at least, and was first printed in Joseph Ritson's *Northumberland Garland* in 1793. In his excellent pamphlet, *Pit Life in Co. Durham* (History Workshop pamphlet no. 6, 1972), David Douglass explains that 'In the early days men half believed that the deeper they mined, the more they were trespassing on territory belonging to the devil'. Later pit legend created the stories of the Big Hewer, a mythical giant of a man who, like Bob Towers of Harraton, was 18 stone of pure muscle. In the words of Jack Elliott of Birtley, Co. Durham: 'The Big Hewer, if he wanted a chew and he hadn't any baccy, he just used to pull a rivet out of the tub and chew it with his fingers . . . He never had a marrow, because there was no one that could keep up with him. A man-and-a-half!' The marrow, variously spelt either marrer or marra, was the workmate, working as a team of two or more. As Douglass explains: 'The miner's wages (and his safety) depend not only on his strength, experience and guts but also on getting good marrows . . . There might be only two marrows to a stall, and even those might work on separate shifts, so that a man only saw his marrow when he came on to relieve him late in the morning. But even if they did not work together, they still shared their earnings.' This is part of the traditional organisation of pitwork that the NCB have been trying to do away with — and the great strike of 1972 was an unexpected by-product of these efforts by the Coal Board. Douglass explains the chorus of the song by saying that 'The miner knew that if his lamp went out all he had to do was to follow the horse for it instinctively knew the road.' A rant is a Northumbrian dance, the most well-known of which is the *Morpeth rant.*

THE COCKFIGHT

Come all ye colliers far and near,
I'll tell of a cock-fight, when and where,
Those Liverpool lads, I heard them say,
Between a black and our bonnie grey.

First come in was the Oldham lads,
They come with all the money they had.
The reason why, they all did say,
The black's too big for the bonnie grey.

It's into the pub to take a sup,
The cock-fight it was soon made up.
For twenty pounds these cocks will play,
The charcoal black and the bonnie grey.

Now when these cocks came to the sod,
Cry the Liverpool lads, How now, what odds?
The odds, the Oldham lads did say,
'Tween the charcoal black and the bonnie grey.

The Oldham lads stood shouting round,
I'll lay you a quid to half a crown,
If our black cock he gets fair play,
He'll clip the wings of the bonnie grey.

So the cocks they at it and the grey was tossed
And the Oldham lads said, Bah, you've lost!
Us collier lads we went right pale,
And we wished we'd fought for a barrel of ale.

And the cocks they at it, one, two, three,
And the charcoal black got struck in the eye.
They picked him up but he would not play,
And the cockfight went to our bonnie grey.

With the silver breast and the silver wing,
He's fit to fight in front of the king,
Hip hip hooray, hooray, hooray!
Away we carried our bonnie grey.

Some old broadsides call this song *The bonny grey*, (often spelt 'gray') in honour of its victorious hero, and have the 12th Earl of Derby wagering ten guineas to a crown against the working class blokes that their cock would lose.

DOWN IN A COALMINE

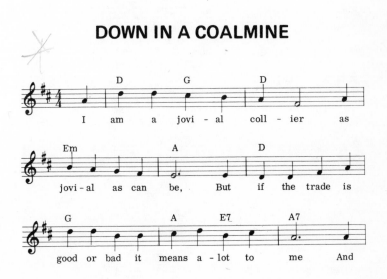

if I stum-ble with my tongue I've one ex-cuse to say, It's not the coll-ier's heart that's wrong, it's the head that goes a - stray. Down in a coal-mine, un-der-neath the ground, Where a gleam of sun-shine's nev-er to be found, Dig-ging dusk-y dia-monds all the sea-son round, Down in a coal-mine un-der-neath the ground.

I am a jovial collier, as jovial as can be,
But if the trade is good or bad it means a lot to me.
And if I stumble with my tongue, I've one excuse to say,
It's not the collier's heart that's wrong, it's the head that goes
    astray.
chorus: Down in a coalmine underneath the ground,
             Where a gleam of sunshine's never to be found,
             Digging dusky diamonds all the season round,
             Down in a coalmine underneath the ground.

How bravely all them collier lads they toil beneath the ground,
Digging for the coal as the days and nights go round,
And anxiously their families wait, how often is it said,
You never know by nightfall how many may be dead.

How little do the rich men care who sit at home secure,
What dangers all the colliers dare, and hardships they endure.
The very fires they have at home to cheer them and their wives
Perhaps were kindled at the cost of jovial colliers' lives.

Originally composed as a stage song by J.B. Geoghegan in 1872,
which is the origin of the occasional lines which do not ring exactly
true to the way pitmen feel about their work, this song has spread
across the world, being as popular among the miners of
Pennsylvania as those of Britain. It is often sung to the tune of *The
roving journeyman,* but I prefer the slower, more melodramatic
melody noted down by George Korson.

SWALWELL HOPPING

words: John Selkirk
tune: *Paddy's wedding*

Lads make a ring and hear us sing The
sport we had___ at Swal - well, oh. Wor
mer - ry play o' the hop -ping day, Ha -whey
mar - rows, and___ I'll tell you, oh. The
sun shines warm on Whick - ham Bank, Let's
all lie doon at Dol - ly's, oh, And
hear 'boot ma - ny a fun - ny prank Played
by the lads at Crow - ley's, oh, Fal

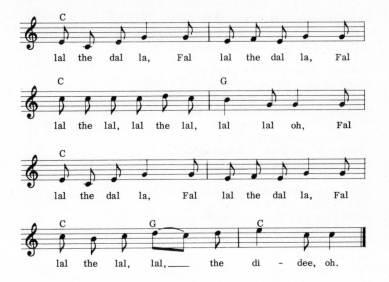

lal the dal la, Fal lal the dal la, Fal
lal the lal, lal the lal, lal lal oh, Fal
lal the dal la, Fal lal the dal la, Fal
lal the lal, lal, ___ the di - dee, oh.

Lads make a ring and hear us sing
The sport we had at Swalwell, oh.
Wor merry play o' the hopping day,
Ha-whey marrows, and I'll tell you, oh.
The sun shines warm on Whickham Bank,
Let's all lie doon at Dolly's, oh,
And hear 'boot many a funny prank
Played by the lads at Crowley's, oh.

There was Sam, oh zoons, with his pantaloons
And cravat up ower his gobby, oh.
And Willie, thoo, with the jacket blue,
Thoo was the very bobby, oh.
There was knock-kneed Mat, with's purple suit
And hopper-hipped Dick, all yellow, oh.
Great Tom was there, with Hepple's old coat,
And buck-sheened Tom from Stella, oh.

When we were dressed it was confessed
We shamed the chaps frae Newcastle, oh.
So away we set to wor toon gate
To jeer them all as passed us, oh.
We shouted some, we some dung doon,

Lobstrop'us fellows we kicked them, oh.
Some culls went home, some crushed to toon,
Some gat aboot by Whickham, oh.

The spree came on, the hat was won
By carrot-powed Jenny's Jackie, oh.
What face, by gock, had buckle-mouthed Jock
When he twined his jaws for the baccy, oh.
The kilted lasses fell to pell-mell
With *Talli-i-o the grinder,* oh.
The smock was given to slavering Nell.
You'd dropped had you been behind her, oh.

Wor dance began, I'd buck-toothed Nan,
And Geordie, thoo'd Jen Collin, oh,
While the merry black with many a crack
Set the tambourine a-rolling, oh.
Like wor forge-hammer, we bet so true,
And shuck Raw's hoose, so soundly, oh.
Tuff canna come up with Crowley's crew
Nor thump the tune so roundly, oh.

Then Gateside Jack with's bloody back
Would dance with goggle-eyed Molly, oh
But up came Nick and gave him a kick
And a canny bit kind of fally, oh.
That day all Hawks's blacks may rue,
They got many a very sore clanker, oh,
Can they do owse with Crowley's crew
From a needle to an anchor, oh.

What's that to say to the bonnie fray
We had with skipper Robin, oh.
The keel bullies all, both great and small
Made beggarly tide of the hopping, oh.
Gleed Will cried, More, up lap old Frank,
And Robin that married his daughter, oh.
We hammered their ribs like an anchor shank,
They found it six weeks after, oh.

Bald-pate John Carr would have a bit spar
To help his marrows away with, oh.
But poor old fellow, he'd gotten ower mellow,
So we dooned both him and Davy, oh.
Then Petticoat Robin jumped up again
With's gully to massacree us, oh.

But Winlaton Dan laid him flat with a stone,
Hurrah for Crowley's crew, boys, oh.

Their hash was sattled so off they rattled
And we jigged it up so hearty, oh,
With many a shiver and lowp so cliver.
Can Newcastle turn out sic a party, oh?
When quite done, ower the fiddlers went,
We staggered a hint so merry, oh,
And through wor toon, till fairly spent,
Roared Crowley's crew and glory, oh.

THE PITMAN'S DOG

words: William Mitford
tune: *The chapter of kings*

In a town near New-cas-tle a
pit-man did dwell With his wife named Peg, a tom-
cat and hiss-el', A dog call-ed Cap-py he
do-ted up-on Be-cause he was left him by
great Un-cle Tom. Well bred Cap-py,

fa-mous old Cap-py, Cap-py's the dog, tall-i - o, tall-i - o!

In a town near Newcastle a pitman did dwell
With his wife, named Peg, a tom-cat, and hissel',
A dog called Cappy he doted upon
Because he was left him by great Uncle Tom.
chorus: Well bred Cappy, famous old Cappy,
      Cappy's the dog, tallio, tallio.

His tail pitcher-handled, his colour jet black,
Just a foot and a half was the length of his back,
His legs seven inches from shoulder to paws,
And his lugs like two dockins hung ower his jaws.

For hunting of vermin reet clever was he
And the house from all robbers his bark would keep free.
Could both fetch and carry, could sit on a stool,
Or, when frisky, would hunt water rats in a pool.

As Ralphie to market one morn did repair,
In his hat-band a pipe, and well-combed was his hair,
Ower his arm hung a basket, thus onward he speels,
And entered Newcastle with Cap at his heels.

He hadn't got farther than foot of the Side
Before he fell in with the dog-killing tribe,
When a highwayman fellow slipped round in a crack
And a thump on the skull laid him flat on his back.
      Down went Cappy, famous old Cappy,
      Cappy's the dog, tallio, tallio.

Now Ralphie, extonished, Cap's fate did repine
While its eyes like two little pearl buttons did shine.
He then spat on his hands, in a fury he grew,
Cries, God smash, but I'se have satisfaction of thoo
      For knocking down Cappy, famous old Cappy,
      Cappy's the dog, tallio, tallio.

Then this grim-looking fellow his bludgeon he raised
When Ralphie eyed Cappy and then stood amazed,
But fearing beside him he might be laid down
Threw him into the basket and banged out of town.

Away went Cappy, famous old Cappy,
Cappy's the dog, tallio, tallio.

He breathless got home and when lifting the sneck
His wife exclaimed, Ralphie, thoo's soon getting back!
Getting back, replies Ralphie, I wish I'd never gyen,
In Newcastle they're felling dogs, lasses, and men.
They've knocked down Cappy, famous old Cappy,
Cappy's the dog, tallio, tallio.

If I gan to Newcastle when comes wor pay week
I'll ken him again by the patch on his cheek.
Or if ever he enters wor town with his stick
We'll thump him about till he's black as old Nick,
For killing old Cappy, famous old Cappy,
Cappy's the dog, tallio, tallio.

With tears in her eyes Peggy heard his sad tale
And Ralph with confusion and terror grew pale.
While Cappy's transactions with grief they talked ower
He crept oot the basket quite brisk on the floor.
Well done Cappy, famous old Cappy,
Cappy's the dog, tallio, tallio.

THE COAL TRADE

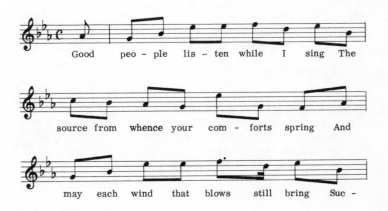

Good peo - ple lis - ten while I sing The

source from whence your com - forts spring And

may each wind that blows still bring Suc -

cess un - to the coal trade. Who

but un - us - ual plea - sure feels To

see our fleets of ships and keels? New -

cas - tle, Sun - der - land and Shields May

ev - er bless the coal trade.

Good people listen while I sing
The source from whence your comforts spring
And may each wind that blows still bring
    Success unto the coal trade.
Who but unusual pleasure feels
To see our fleets of ships and keels?
Newcastle, Sunderland and Shields
    May ever bless the coal trade.

What is it gives us cakes of meal?
What is it crams our wames so weel
With lumps of beef and draughts of ale?
    What is't but just the coal trade?
Not Davis Straits, nor Greenland oil,
Nor all the wealth springs from the soil
Could ever make our pots to boil
    Like unto our coal trade.

Ye sailors' wives that love a drop
Of stingo from the brandy shop
How could you get one single drop
     If it were not for the coal trade?
Ye pitman lads, so blithe and gay,
Who meet to tipple each payday,
Down on your marrowbones and pray
     Success unto the coal trade.

This nation is in duty bound
To prize those who work underground
For 'tis well known this country round
     Is kept up by the coal trade.
May Wear and Tyne and Thames ne'er freeze,
Our ships and keels will pass with ease,
Then Newcastle, Sunderland and Shields
     Will still uphold the coal trade.

I tell the truth you may depend:
In Durham or Northumberland
No trade in them could ever stand
     If it were not for the coal trade.
The owners know full well, 'tis true,
Without pitmen, keelmen, sailors too,
To Britain they might bid adieu
     If it were not for the coal trade.

So to conclude and make an end
Of these few lines which I have penned,
We'll drink a health to all these men
     Who carry on the coal trade.
To owners, pitmen, keelmen too,
And sailors, who the seas do plough,
Without these men we could not do,
     Nor carry on the coal trade.

Full of Victorian confidence, this north-eastern song comes from John Stokoe's pioneer collection, *Songs and Ballads of Northern England*. The various 'farewells' of a century later, as the National Coal Board closes pits that still have coal in them to be mined, tell a different story — and, between them, these songs tell of the rise and fall of industrialism.

MY LAD'S A CANNY LAD

Saw ye owt of my lad gan-ning
doon the wag-gon__ way With his
poc-ket full of mon-ey and his
poke full of hay? Oh my lad's a can-ny__ lad the
can-ni-est I see With his
fine pos-ey waist-coat and__ buck-les at his knee.

Saw ye owt of my lad ganning doon the waggon way
With his pocket full of money and his poke full of hay?
    Oh, my lad's a canny lad, the canniest I see,
    With his fine posey waistcoat and buckles at his knee.

There's never a lad like my lad drives to the staiths on Tyne,
He's coaly-black on workdays but on holidays he's fine.
    Oh, my lad's a bonnie lad, the bonniest I see,
    And never a one there is could say that black is in his ee.

With his siller in his hand and with love in his ee,
Yonder I see my canny lad a-coming doon to me.
     Aye but he's a bonnie laddie as ever ye did see,
     Though he's sair pock-brocken and he's blind of an ee.

Rivals to the keelmen were the waggoners, who pushed the carts of coals along railed tracks before the invention of the steam engine. When John Bell noted it, he gave no indication of tune, but the one most used in the coalfields today, where the song is still sung, is a variant of the extremely widespread *Ball of Kirriemuir*. The famous Elliott family of Birtley have a ribald parody:

    Oh my lad's a canny lad, he works down the pit,
    He never comes to see us unless he wants a bit.
    I asked him would he marry us, you should have seen him
       wince.
    I think I've lost my canny lad, I've never seen him since.

FOOTY AGAINST THE WALL

the   Moor Yate   play foot-y   a-gainst   the   wa'._____

From Benton Bank to Benton town there's not a pitman's raw,
So when you get to the Moor Yate play footy against the wa'.

Chorus: Then hie footy and how footy and footy against the wa'.
          And when you get to the Moor Yate, play footy against
          the wa'.

The wife went down the Moor Lonnin and let her basket fa'.
For when she gat to the Moor Yate, played footy against the wa'.

The stoby road's a stoby place and some of the stobs are law,
But still there's some that's high enough for footy against the wa'.

The Holy Stone's a holy place, the trees are thick and law,
But they are nought to the Moor Yate for footy against the wa'.

Wapping Square is a bonnie place, the houses are but sma',
But in them yet there's room enough for footy against the wa'.

The lady did not like the house, for the air it was too raw,
It was sweeter far at the Moor Yate for footy against the wa'.

Young Cuddy is a bonnie lad and Robin's tall and sma',
But if you come to wor town end they'll footy against the wa'.

When Frank Graham put this in his *Geordie Song Book* of 1971 he
commented: 'A song much sung many years ago, by the pitmen
about Long Benton. First published in Bell's *Rhymes of the
Northern Bards,* 1812, but not published again because of
Victorian prudery. The word 'footy' is an amorous term of French
origin.' Actually, it is derived from foutre, meaning to fuck.

THE PITMAN'S HAPPY TIMES

words: James Robson
tune: *The days when we went gypsying*

When I was young my coll - ier lads no
man could hap - pier be, For wages was like
small coals then, and chaps could raise a
spree. Wor pay - neet came with drink and dance, wor
sweet - hearts looked so fine, And lumps of beef and
dads of duff was there for folks to dine. And
then we spent sic mer- ry neets for grum-bling we had
nane, But the times of wor pros - per - i - ty will

ne - ver come a - gain. But the times of wor pro -

sper - i - ty will nev - er come a - gain.

When I was young, my collier lads, no man could happier be,
For wages was like small coals then, and chaps could raise a spree.
Wor pay-neet came with drink and dance, wor sweethearts looked
    so fine,
And lumps of beef and dads of duff was there for folks to dine.
And then we spent sic merry neets, for grumbling we had nane,
But the times of wor prosperity will never come again.

Wor hooses then was ower small, for every nook was chock,
Wor drawers was fair mahogany and so was chairs and clock.
Wor feather beds and powls so fine was welcome to the seet,
A man worked harder in the day with thinking of the neet.
Spice hinnies on the girdle fixed, my tea had rum in't then,
But the times of wor prosperity will never come again.

Wor wives could buy new shawls and goons and never heed the
    price.
The spyed-yece guineas went like smoke to make wor darlings nice.
The drapers used no tickets then the country gowks to coax.
They got directly what was asked and praised us collier folks.
The butcher meat was always best when Kenton paid their men,
But the days of wor prosperity can never come again.

When I got wed, gocks what a row, the binding brass was spent.
I bought new gloves and ribbons, man, for all the folks I kent.
At every ale hoose in this toon we had a cocktail pot,
With treating all the company roond my kelter went like shot.
But, smash, we had a merry neet, though fights we had but ten,
There was sic times for collier lads — they'll never come again.

We didn't heed much learning then, we had no time for school.
Pit laddies worked for spending's sake and none was thought a
    fool.
Now every bairn can read and write, extonishing to me.

The very dowpie on my lap can tell his A.B.C.
Some folk gets reet and some gets wrong by letting books alane,
But this I'll swear, no times like mine can ever come again.

Robson was one of the oldest of the Tyneside bards. He was a
musician in the Jacobite army of 1715 and was imprisoned in
Preston, where he made up songs and sang them through the bars
of the jail to get money to keep from starving.

THE PITMAN'S LOVESONG

I wish my love was a scarlet cherry
And growing on yon cherry tree
And I myself was a bonnie blackbird,
How would I peck that red cherry!

I wish my love was a red, red rose
And growing on yon garden wall
And I myself was a drop of dew,
Oh on that red rose would I fall.

I wish my love she was a fish
And swimming in the salt, salt sea
And I myself was a fisher lad,
How would I play with her reet cunningly!

I wish my love was in a kist
And I myself to hold the key
Then would I gan tin her when I had list
And keep my hinny good company.

I wish my love was an old grey mare
And grazing by yon riverside
And I myself was a bonnie saddle,
Oh on that old grey mare how would I ride!

I wish my love was a bell beehive
And I myself was a humble bee
That I might come and creep into her
And gorge myself of her sweet honey.

I wish my love was a ripe turd
And smoking down in yon dykeside
And I myself was a shitten flea,
I'd suck her up before she dried.

My love she's fair, she's very fair,
She's from Newcastle born and bred.
Her skin it is a lily white,
Her cheeks they are such a rosy red.

My love she's bonnie, she's wondrous canny,
And she's well fair-ed for to see.
As I think on, my love's upon her,
Under her apron fain would I be.

These magic words, taken originally from John Bell's manuscript collection but changed even more than usual in the process of singing by me, have always lacked a tune. I myself set them to a version of *Lord Bateman* which Grainger collected on a phonograph cylinder from the great Joseph Taylor and recently recorded by Steve Ashley. When A.L. Lloyd recorded them he used another tune. But at last I may have found the clue in some words which Sam Henry found in the notebooks of an Irish choirsinger, William Robb. It seems that some religious folk felt it sacrilegious to sing the sacred words of the psalms on any occasion but the church service, and so at choir practice they would substitute secular words; something similar happened in Scotland. Among the words in Mr Robb's choirbook were something very like our first verse (though with no specific psalm tune attached) plus paraphrases of verses from the *Song of Solomon* which, though they lack the erotic similes that also appealed to the compiler of *Pills to Purge Melancholy*, are in a somewhat similar vein. This, for instance, to the tune, *Martyrs*:

> *I'll marble wall thee round about,*
> *Myself shall be the door,*
> *And if your heart chance to break out*
> *I'll never leave thee more.*

(Surely that should be 'never love thee more' — but that is the way Henry copies it.) And this, to the tune *York*:

> *My love, my dove, my undefiled,*
> *My colo do not slight,*
> *My head is wat'red with the dew,*
> *With dropping of the night.*

If the whole song is meant to be sung to a psalm tune one's mind nevertheless boggles at the vision of a collier church choir bawling out our seventh verse of which the normally unfastidious Lloyd confesses, in the note to his recording (on Topic 12T118), 'Rather to my own surprise I find myself too prudish to sing it, though I'm impressed by its intensity'. The tune printed here is adapted from Taylor's *Bateman*. For another industrial song to a psalm tune, see *Surat warps*.

THE PITMAN'S COURTSHIP

by William Mitford

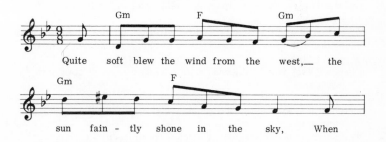

Quite soft blew the wind from the west,— the sun fain-tly shone in the sky, When

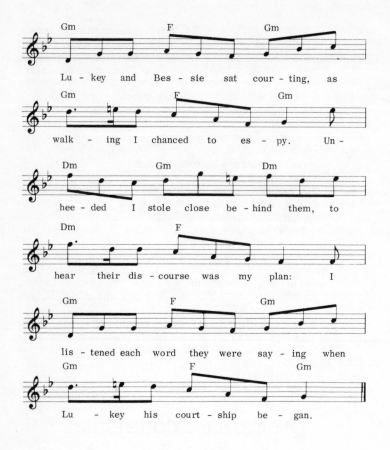

Gm   F   Gm

Lu - key and Bes - sie sat cour - ting, as

Gm   F   Gm

walk - ing I chanced to es - py. Un -

Dm   Gm   Dm

hee - ded I stole close be - hind them, to

Dm   F

hear their dis - course was my plan: I

Gm   F   Gm

lis - tened each word they were say - ing when

Gm   F   Gm

Lu - key his court - ship be - gan.

Quite soft blew the wind from the west, the sun faintly shone in
      the sky,
When Lukey and Bessie sat courting, as walking I chanced to espy.
Unheeded I stole close behind them, to hear their discourse was
      my plan:
I listened each word they were saying when Lukey his courtship
      began.

Last hopping thou won up my fancy with thy fine silken jacket
      of blue
And smash if the fine Newcastle ladies could marrow the curls of
      thy broo.

That day I whiles danced with long Nancy, she couldn't like thou
    lift her heel.
My grandy likes spice singing hinnies, my comely, I like thou as
    weel.

Thou knows, ever since we were little, together we've ranged
    through the woods,
At nights hand-in-hand toddled home, very oft with howl kites and
    torn duds.
But now we can talk about marriage and long sair for wor wedding
    day,
When married we'll keep a bit shop and sell things in a huckstery
    way.

And to get us a canny bit living, all kinds of sweetmeats we'll sell:
Red herring, brown syrup, and mint candy, black pepper, dye sand,
    and small yell,
Spice hunters, pick shafts, farthing candles, wax dollies with red
    leather shoes,
Chalk pussy cats, fine curly greens, paper skates, penny pies and
    huil-doos.

I'se help thou to tie up the sugar at nights when frae work I get
    lowse
And wor Dick that lives ower by High Whickham, he'll make us
    broom besoms for nowse.
Like an image thou's stand ower the counter with thy fine muslin,
    cambricker goon,
And to let folks see thou's a lady on a cuddy thou's ride to the
    toon.

There's be matches, pipe clay, and broon dishes, canary seed,
    raisins, and fegs,
And to please the pit laddies at Easter, a dishful of giltey paste-eggs.
Wor neighbours, that's snuffers and smokers, for wor snuff and
    wor baccy they'll seek,
And to show them we deal with Newcastle, twee blackies shall
    mense the door cheek.

So now for Tim Bodkin I'se send to darn my silk breeks at the knee.
Thou thy ruffles and frills mun get ready, next Whit-Sunday
    married we'll be.
Now I think it's high time to be stepping, we've sitting till I'se
    about lame.
So then with a kiss and a cuddle these lovers they bent their ways
    hame.

William Mitford was born in North Shields in 1788 and died in Newcastle in 1851. I wonder how many of the goodies he lists are on sale now. My granny always used to be partial to a mint humbug called 'black bullets' but so far as I know it's not sold on Tyneside any more though, to many, boiled sweets are still all called bullets.

WITH MY PIT BOOTS ON

A-digging and a-picking as I was one day,
The thought of my true love it led me astray.
The shift being over and the night coming on,
So away I ran with my pitboots on.

I went to my love's window crying, Are you in bed?
The minute that she heard me she lifted up her head,
She lifted up her head and she said, Is that John?
Indeed it's me with my pitboots on.

She came to the door and invited me in,
Draw near to the fire and warm up your skin.
The bedroom door it opened and the blanket it turned down
And I rolled into bed with my pitboots on.

We tossed and we tumbled until the break of day,
Not thinking of the hours that we had spent in play,
Till my love she jumped up, crying, Oh what have we done?
The baby will come with his pitboots on.

I chastised my love for talking so wild,
You foolish young girl, you will never have a child,
For all that we done it was only done in fun,
But away I ran with my pitboots on.

So come all you young maidens wherever that you be,
Don't never let a collier lad an inch above your knee,
For their hearts do run old and their heads do run young,
So look out for the fellows with their pitboots on.

Apart from the change of occupation, the words of this miner's
song, popularised by A.L. Lloyd, are almost identical with a similar
song about a man who never took off his kettle smock, which Cecil
Sharp collected from William Stokes of Chew Magna, Somerset, in
January 1907. Other versions, in which it is called a *courting*
smock (and according to Partridge, kettle is an archaic word for
cunt), have been collected in Westmorland and Shetland. See also
The bold Irish navvy.

THE KEEL ROW

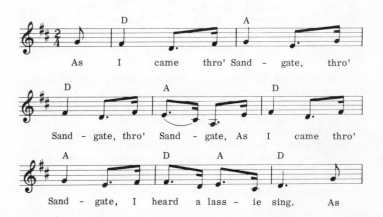

As I came through Sandgate, through Sandgate, through Sandgate,
As I came through Sandgate I heard a lassie sing.
As I came through Sandgate, through Sandgate, through Sandgate,
As I came through Sandgate I heard a lassie sing:
chorus: Weel may the keel row, the keel row, the keel row,
Weel may the keel row that my laddie's in.
And weel may the keel row, the keel row, the keel row,
Weel may the keel row that my laddie's in.

He wears a blue bonnet, blue bonnet, blue bonnet,
He wears a blue bonnet and a dimple in his chin.
He wears a blue bonnet, blue bonnet, blue bonnet,
He wears a blue bonnet and a dimple in his chin.

Whae's like my Johnny, so leish, so blithe, so bonnie?
He's foremost 'mong the mony keel lads of coaly Tyne.
Whae's like my Johnny, so leish, so blithe, so bonnie?
He's foremost 'mong the mony keel lads of coaly Tyne.

He'll set and row so lightly or in the dance so sprightly,
He'll cut and shuffle sightly, 'tis true were he not mine.
He'll set and row so lightly or in the dance so sprightly,
He'll cut and shuffle sightly, 'tis true were he not mine.

May all the press gangs perish, each lass her laddie cherish,
Long may the coal trade flourish upon the coaly Tyne.
May all the press gangs perish, each lass her laddie cherish,
Long may the coal trade flourish upon the coaly Tyne.

And now he's in the union, the union, the union,
And now he's in the union, my bonnie Johnny lad.
And now he's in the union, the union, the union,
And now he's in the union, my bonnie Johnny lad.

The word 'keel' is from an Anglo-Saxon derivation, meaning ship, but on the Tyne and Wear it was applied to a clumsy great oval, flat-bottomed boat used for carrying 20 tons of coal at a time from the dykes or staiths upriver to the collier ships at berth in the harbour. According to Maxine Baker, 'The boat was steered by two men known as 'keel bullies'. They used a large oar at the stern which was called a 'swarpe'. A pole with an iron point was used in shallow water — called a 'set' on the Wear and a 'pug' on the Tyne. They would walk up and down the boat wielding these and pushing the boat along, in a similar way to that used in punts. The keelmen were famous for their hard lives, drinking and knocking their wives around.' Hence *The Sandgate lass's lamentation*. Most of the verses were first printed by John Bell in 1812, including the third, fourth and fifth printed here, which he got from a timber merchant called Thomas Thompson. The last verse is of Twentieth Century origin, though despite the old song which used *as lang as keel gans down River Tyne* as a metaphor for eternity, the keels have not plied for a century or more.

CUSHIE BUTTERFIELD

words: George Ridley
tune: *Pretty Polly Perkins of Paddington Green*

I's a brok-en heart-ed keel-man and I's ow-er heid in love With a young lass in Gate-side and I call her my dove, Her name's Cush-ie But-ter-field and she sells yel-low clay, And her cou-sin is a muck man and they call him Tom Grey. She's a big lass and a bon-nie lass And she likes her beer, And they call her Cush-ie But-ter-field And I wish she was here.

I's a broken-hearted keelman and I's ower heid in love
With a young lass in Gateside and I call her my dove,
Her name's Cushie Butterfield and she sells yellow clay,
And her cousin is a muckman and they call him Tom Grey.

chorus: She's a big lass and a bonnie lass
          And she likes her beer,
          And they call her Cushie Butterfield
          And I wish she was here.

Her eyes is like two holes in a blanket burnt through,
Her brows in a morning would spyen a young cow,
And when I hear her shoutin, Will ye buy any clay?
Like a candyman's trumpet, it steals my heart away.

You'll oft see her down at Sandgate when the fresh herring comes
        in,
She's like a bag full of sawdust tied round with a string.
She wears big galoshes tae, and her stockings once was white,
And her petticoat's violet and her hat's never straight.

When I axed her to marry me she started to laugh,
Noo, none of your monkey tricks for I like nae such chaff.
Then she started a-bubbling and she roared like a bull,
And the chaps on the Quay says I's nowt but a fool.

She says the chap that gets her must work every day,
And when he comes home at neets he must gan and seek clay.
And when he's away seeking she'll make balls and sing:
Oh weel may the keel row that my laddie's in.

Ridley was a Tyneside comedian, an ex-collier who was only 30
when he died in 1864. The word 'spyen' in line two of verse two
means to dry up the milk. Although I have sung this for years, I
had to consult a dialect dictionary before I could translate some of
the words of the original into standard English.

THE SANDGATE LASS

words: Robert Nunn
tune: *Fy let us a' to the Bridal*

On the Ro - pery Banks Jin-ny was sit -ting She had on a bed goon just new. And blithe - ly the las - sie was knit -ting With yarn of a bon - nie sky__ blue The strings of her cap they were hang - ing So long on her shoul - ders so fine And hear - ty I heard this lass sing - ing My bon - nie keel lad shall be mine. Oh

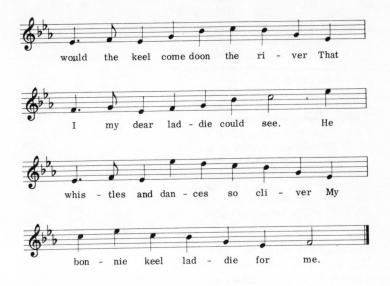

would the keel come doon the ri - ver That
I my dear lad - die could see. He
whis - tles and dan - ces so cli - ver My
bon - nie keel lad - die for me.

On the Ropery Banks Jinny was sitting,
She had on a bed-goon just new,
And blithely the lassie was knitting
With yarn of a bonnie sky-blue.
The strings of her cap they were hanging
So long on her shoulders so fine
And hearty I heard this lass singing,
My bonnie keel lad shall be mine.
chorus: Oh would the keel come doon the river
That I my dear laddie could see.
He whistles and dances so cliver,
My bonnie keel laddie for me.

Last neet in among these green dockins
He fed me with gingerbread spice.
I promised to knit him these stockings,
He cuddled and kissed me so nice.
He called me his jewel and his hinny,
He called me his pet and his bride,
And he swore that I should be his Jinny,
To lie at neets doon by his side.

That morning forget I will never
When first I saw him on the Quay.

The *Keel row* he whistled so cliver,
He won my affections from me.
His drawers on his doup looked so canny,
His keel hat was cocked on his head,
And if I'd not gotten my Jimmy,
Faith, by this time I would been dead.

The first time I spoke to my Jimmy,
Now mind ye, it isn't a lee,
My mother had gi'en me a penny
To bring her a pennorth of tea,
When a lad in the street cried out, Bessie!
Says I, Hinny, that's not my name.
Becrike, never mind, he says. Lassie
Toneet I will see you safe hame.

Since then I have been his true lover,
I've loved him as dear as my life,
And in spite of both father and mother
I'll soon be my keel-laddie's wife.
How happy we'll be then together
When he brings hame his wages to me,
With his bonnie bit bairn crying, Father,
And another one laid on my knee.

In Lloyd's *Come All Ye Bold Miners,* where I first found this song,
he says it should be sung to the tune of *The skipper's wedding* but
I think he errs there. The tune in Allan's *Tyneside Songs* of 1891 is
as given here.

THE SANDGATE GIRL'S
LAMENTATION

tune: *The Manchester 'Angel'*

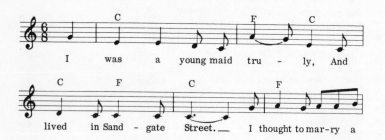

good___ man to keep me warm at neet.___ He's an ug - ly bo - dy a bub - bly bo - dy An ill fared hid - e - ous loon.___ Since I mar-ried a keel - man, All my good days are done.___

I was a young maid truly, and lived in Sandgate Street.
I thought to marry a good man to keep me warm at neet.
chorus: He's an ugly body, a bubbly body,
An ill-fared hideous loon.
Since I have married a keelman
All my good days are done.

I thought to marry a parson to hear me say my prayers
But I have married a keelman and he kicks me doon the stairs.

I thought to marry a dyer to dye my apron blue
But I have married a keelman and he makes me sorely rue.

I thought to marry a joiner to make me chair and stool
But I have married a keelman and he's a perfect fool.

I thought to marry a sailor to bring me sugar and tea
But I have married a keelman and that he lets me see.

The words, with no tune given, were first printed by John Bell in 1812. In 1888 Joseph Crawhall printed it again, with this tune, which is the way we used to sing it when I was a kid in Whitley Bay, though I think our source was originally a school songbook that one of our elders had.

SANDGATE DANDLING SONG

words: Robert Nunn
tune: *Dollia*

Ah you are my bonnie bairn, ah you are upon my arm,
Ah you are, thou soon may learn to say Dada, sae canny.
I wish thy daddy may be weel, he's lang in coming frae the keel,
Though his black face is like the deil, I like a kiss frae Johnny.

Thou really has thy daddy's chin, thou art like him, leg and wing,
And I with pleasure can thee sing since thou belongs my Johnny.
Johnny is a clever lad, last neet he fuddled all he had.
This morning he wasn't verry bad, he looked as blithe as ony.

Though thou's the first, thou's not the last, I mean to hae my
      bairns fast
And when this happy time is past I still will love my Johnny.
For his hair is broon and so is thine, thine eyes are grey and so are
      mine.
Thy nose is tapered off so fine, thou's like thy daddy, Johnny.

Thy canny dowp is fat and roond, and like thy dad, thou's plump
      and soond.
Thou's worth to me a thousand poond, thou's altogether bonnie.
When daddy's drunk he'll take a knife and threatens sair to take
      my life,
Who wouldn't be a keelman's wife to have a man like Johnny?

But yonder's daddy coming now, he looks the best among the
      crew.
They're all gone to the Barley Mow, my canny good-like Johnny.
Come, let's now get the bacon fried and let us make a clean
      fireside,
Then on his knee he will thee ride when he comes hame to mammy.

The words by the blind fiddler of Tyneside were first printed in
1842, but the tune is much older. It was taken by the Merseyside
songwriter Stan Kelly for a clever parody which has been recorded
by such different singers as Cilla Black and Judy Collins, but it has
the gritty realism of Nunn's song, still intact.

FOURPENCE A DAY

by Thomas Raine

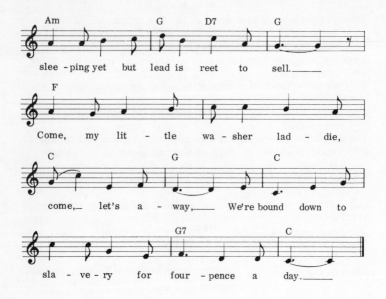

slee-ping yet but lead is reet to sell.

Come, my lit - tle wa - sher lad - die,

come,_ let's a - way,___ We're bound down to

sla - ve - ry for four - pence a day.___

The ore is waiting in the tubs, the snow's upon the fell.
Canny folk are sleeping yet but lead is reet to sell.
Come my little washer laddie, come let's away,
We're bound down to slavery for fourpence a day.

It's early in the morning we rise at five o'clock,
And the little slaves come to the door to knock, knock, knock.
Come my little washer laddie, come let's away,
It's very hard to work for fourpence a day.

My father was a miner and lived down in the town,
'Twas hard work and poverty that always kept him down.
He aimed for me to go to school but brass he couldn't pay,
So I had to go to the washing rig for fourpence a day.

My mother rises out of bed with tears upon her cheek,
Puts my wallet on my shoulders which has to serve a week.
It often fills her heart with woe when she unto me doth say,
I never thought thou would have worked for fourpence a day.

Fourpence a day, my lad, and very hard to work,
And ne'er a pleasant look from a gruffy looking Turk.
His conscience it may fail him, his heart it may give way,
Then he'll raise us our wages to ninepence a day.

For some reason the logic of which I have been unable to discover, the earliest legislation curbing the employment of child labour specifically excluded the mines, with the result that the Mines Commission of 1842 disclosed that since 1833 the numbers of children employed in the mines had actually increased, especially in Lancashire and the West Riding of Yorkshire. This is commemorated in a verse that forms part of a 'nominy' still chanted by the kids of Sowerby Bridge on 'Plot Night', November 5:

> *Little lad in't coil pit goes knock knock knock*
> *And when he's done his work he peeps out o'top.*

This song actually stems from the lead mines, where conditions underground were so bad that generally women and children were kept on the surface washing the slack out of the ore. It was obtained of Mr John Gowland, a retired leadminer, of Middleton-in-Teesdale in Yorkshire.

LITTLE CHANCE

I had a lit - tle Gall - ow - ay, his
name was Lit - tle Chance,— He used to make the
full 'uns— fly and make the chum - mins
dance, And it was lowse off the lim - bers— turn
loose and hing him on Din - na for - get to

tok - en and twine at twists and turns.___

I had a little Galloway, his name was Little Chance,
He used to make the full 'uns fly and make the chummins dance.
And it was lowse off the limbers, turn loose and hing him on,
Dinna forget to token and twine at twists and turns.

So it was in and out, all day long, heck, see and get away.
You had no time to lie around, when slushin' for some pay.
Now Chancey had two greasy legs and a kettley back,
And up and down the gannin' board he made the tubs to knack.

He also tore around the turns, you couldn't hold him back,
And if you didn't twine in time the tub got off the track.
I mind the time at the S-turn, the closen joint I missed.
The tub it dropped off all fours and smashed the deputy's kist.

There came a day I'll never forget, although I'm old and grey,
The wooden sprag it did smash, and the hitch tub got away.
Down the heavy it did fly, there was a mighty smash.
The tub it finished upside down on me and Chancey both.

The boss he called the overman in the happenings to relate,
And when he heard that Chance was dead it made him twist his
      face:
I know the lad was badly hurt, he was a stretcher case,
But Galloways like Little Chance are harder to replace.

Certainly the origin of the well-known but fragmentary comic song
of the same name as sung by Jack Elliott, Bob Davenport and
others, this was collected by Maxine Baker from Mr J. Hutchinson
of Bowburn who says he learned it down Lambton 'D' pit in 1915.
Galloway pit ponies no longer work underground, but in those
days they were reckoned to be more valuable than a miner's life, as
the callous last verse indicates.

188

LITTLE CHANCE

good, Tit-ty fa la, tit-ty fa lay. I came oot to get a shaft,__ The tim-ber it gave a crack, When a stone fell on my back, Tit-ty fa la, tit-ty fa lay__ Tra la la-la-la la, ow-er the wall's oot.__

You gan ower the busty fields to gan down the pit,
You get your lamp out, you gan inbye, and there you sit at the
 kist.
The deputy says, Thy place is holed, thou'll have to gan straight
 on.
I says to him, What's the matter wi' my own? He says, She canna
 gan on.
        I filled sixteen out of a judd,
        Titty fa la, titty fa lay,
        Eh by hell she was good,
        Titty fa la, titty fa lay.
        I came oot to get a shaft,
        The timber it gave a crack,
        When a stone fell on my back,
        Titty fa la, titty fa lay.
Tra la la-la-la la, ower the wall's oot.

Now Jack and Bill two marrows were, in a public house,
The talk about the cavills, lads, it wouldn't frighten a mouse.
Jack says to Bill, By gock she's hard,
The tops is like bell metal but the bottoms is not so bad.
      Bugger I only got ten the day,
      Titty fa la, titty fa lay,
      I only got ten the day,
      Titty fa la, titty fa lay.
      I would have gotten the other four,
      I was wishing the shift was ower,
      When the putter got off the way,
      Titty fa la, titty fa lay.
Tra la la-la-la la, ower the wall's oot.

Now you're sure to ken my brother Bill, he's so full of wit,
He's got a job of putting, up at the 'Cotia pit,
Now when Bill comes home from work he's like a droonded rat,
Instead of ganning upstairs to bed he lies upon the mat.
      Bugger he puts a thousand or more,
      Titty fa la, titty fa lay,
      They pay him by the score,
      Titty fa la, titty fa lay.
      He fills his tubs so quick,
      Without any delay,
      But he can never find his pick,
      Titty fa la, titty fa lay.
Tra la la-la-la la, ower the wall's oot.

Now my name is Jackie Robinson, the same I do advance,
I drive a little Gallowa', his name is Little Chance.
Chancey has two greasy feet, likewise a kittley back,
And ganning along the ganning-board he makes the chummins knack.
      I was ganning around the turn,
      Titty fa la, titty fa lay,
      Chancey wouldn't had on,
      Titty fa la, titty fa lay.
      The tubs they give a click,
      I got off the way at the switch,
      Ye bugger, I smashed the deputy's kist,
      Titty fa la, titty fa lay.
Fa la la-la-la la, ower the wall's oot.

I'm ganning to put next quarter to make three pounds of pay,
It's better than driving Chancey for eighteen pence a day.
So come all you jolly driver lads, put on your limmers and gan,
And work for Mr Hindley, for he's a gentleman.
(no chorus)

I know a simple maiden and she has a lot of charm,
She asked me aroond to have a look at her little country farm.
She showed me all her pigs and her hens that never laid
And she's ganning to show me something more if I stop for a cup
     of tea.
       So I put my hand upon her calves,
       Titty fa la, titty fa lay,
       She says, Divn't do things by halves,
       Titty fa la, titty fa lay.
       Noo I keep her company,
       Because she's very fond of me,
       And I'm a bugger for tea,
       Titty fa la, titty fa lay.
Tra la la-la-la la, ower the wall's oot.

I know a simple maiden and her age was forty four,
She never had been married but just the night before,
       She thought she heard a noise,
       Titty fa la, titty fa lay,
       It was a burglar under the bed,
       Titty fa la, titty fa lay.
       She didn't shout nor scream,
       But she crept out of her bed,
       And she went to lock the door,
       Titty fa la, titty fa lay.
Tra la la-la-la la, ower the wall's oot.

Now me and my wife and my mother-in-law, we went to the silvery
     sea,
My mother-in-law got into a boat, a sailor she would be.
She hadn't gone but twenty yards when all of a sudden's a shout.
My mother-in-law's in the water and there she's splashing about.
       She says, Help I cannot swim,
       Titty fa la, titty fa lay.
       I says, Now's your chance to learn,
       Titty fa la, titty fa lay.
       My wife she says, Ye hound,
       You're not gonna watch her drown.
       I says, No, I'll shut my eyes,
       Titty fa la, titty fa lay.
Tra la la-la-la la, ower the wall's oot.

As we can see, the song has come a long way from the story of the
pitman and his pony, though the vestiges of the original remain.

The last three verses are very recent, being based on traditional music hall rather than folk themes, though I have heard two of them sung by more than one Durham miner (Billy Hutchinson and Jack Elliott). Charles Bevil of Tow Law, Co. Durham, from whom one of the earliest versions (and our fifth verse) was obtained in 1951 says that the song used to be performed to accompany the old tup, a ceremonial beast constructed from a pig-killing cradle, muslin stretched over a wicker frame, an animal's head, and stubs of candles lit round it, which the pit boys paraded round the village on Christmas Eve, collecting pennies in the trough meant to catch the blood of the pig. A 'tup' is a sheep (in many parts of the country a similar custom is accompanied by the well-known and virile *Derby ram*) but it's not clear whether the beast of Tow Law was meant to be a sheep, a pig or a pit pony. Possibly a bit of all three.

JOWL, JOWL AND LISTEN

Pit wark's more than hew-ing.———— You've got to coax the coal a-long And not be ri-ving and te-wing.————

chorus: Jowl, jowl and listen lad,
        And hear that coalface working.
        There's many a marrow missing lad
        Because he wouldn't listen, lad.

My father always used to say
Pit wark's more than hewing.
You've got to coax the coal along
And not be riving and tewing.

Noo the deputy crawls frae flat to flat
While the putter rams the chummins.
But the man at the face has to know his place
Like a mother knows her young 'uns.

Another authentic piece of coalface folklore collected by Walter Toyn from Henry Nattress. To 'jowl' is to knock at the roof and listen to the sound; an experienced miner can tell from the sound whether the roof is to be trusted.

RAP HER TO BANK

chorus: Rap her to bank, my canny lad.
Wind her away, keep turning.
The back-shift men are ganning hame,
We'll be back here in the morning.

My father used to call the turn
When the long shift was ower.
And ganning outbye you'd hear him cry,
D'ye knaa it's after fower?
      Rap her to bank, my canny lad.
      Wind her away, keep turning.
      The back-shift men are ganning hame,
      We'll be back here in the morning.

And when that awful day arrived,
The last shift for my father,
A fall of stones and broken bones,
But still above the clatter, he cried,
      Rap her to bank, my canny lad,
      Wind her reet slow, that's clever.
      This poor old lad has taken bad.
      I'll be back here never.

In the old days pitmen would rap from the pit-bottom to signal for
the cage to be wound up to the bank (surface) by means of a
rapper-rope, hanging down the shaft and attached to the rapper at
the top. The song seems to have originated in either Hetton-le-Hole
or the Elemore Colliery, both in Co. Durham. A schoolmaster
called Henry Nattress learned the song from his uncle, who had
worked in both, and taught it to another teacher, Walter Toyn of
Birtley, who, incidentally, contributed the fourth line of the
second verse. Frank Rutherford got it from Mr Toyn, but, like so
many fine miners' songs, it became best known through the singing
of Jack Elliott of Birtley.

THE CELEBRATED WORKING MAN

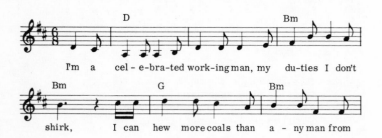

I'm a cel-e-bra-ted work-ing man, my du-ties I don't
shirk, I can hew more coals than a - ny man from

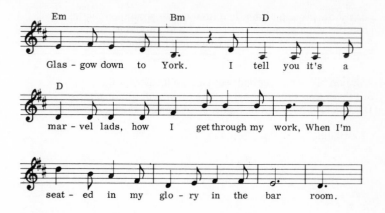

Glas - gow down to York. I tell you it's a
mar - vel lads, how I get through my work, When I'm
seat - ed in my glo - ry in the bar room.

I'm a celebrated working man, my duties I don't shirk,
I can hew more coals than any man from Glasgow down to York.
I tell you it's a marvel, lads, how I get through my work,
When I'm seated in my glory in the bar room.

chorus: In the bar room, in the bar room, that's where we congregate
        To drill the holes and fill the coals and shovel back the
           slate,
        And for to do a job of work I am never late,
        That's provided that we do it in the bar room.

At putting I'm a dandy, I hope you will agree,
And ganning along the ganning board I make the chummins flee.
Your Kelly sweeps and back-ower turns they never bother me
When I'm sitting on the limmers in the bar room.

I can stand a set of timber, post or bar or single prop,
I can cut my juds at the bottom, I can cut them at the top.
Just hand me doon my pick, my lads, and gocks, I winnot stop,
Till I land a set of trams reet in the bar room.

I can judge a shot of powder to a sixteenth of a grain,
I can fill my eighteen tubs though the water falls like rain.
And if you'd like to see me in the perpendicular vein,
It's when I'm setting timbers in the bar room.

I can work a two-foot seam and never be delayed.
Of fire or flood or gas, my lads, I've never been afraid,
And I can show the manager how to go aboot his trade,
And haven't I always proved it in the bar room?

I can show the superintendent how the air should circulate,
I can show the engineman how the steam should generate,
And the trouble at the Chow Dene pit I can elucidate,
And haven't I often done it in the bar room?

And noo my song is ended, perhaps we'll have another,
But don't you fire no shots in here or we will surely smother,
The landlord here would sooner serve himself than go to all the
  bother
Of installing ventilators in the bar room.

THE ROW BETWEEN THE CAGES

words: Thomas Armstrong
tune: *Robin Tamson's smiddy*

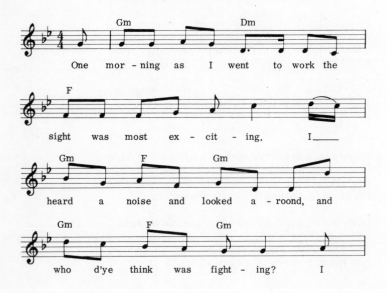

One mor - ning as I went to work the

sight was most ex - cit - ing. I___

heard a noise and looked a - roond, and

who d'ye think was fight - ing? I

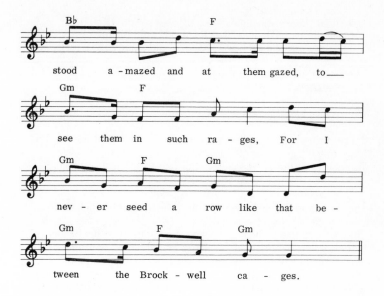

stood a-mazed and at them gazed, to see them in such ra-ges, For I nev-er seed a row like that be-tween the Brock-well ca-ges.

One morning as I went to work, the sight was most exciting.
I heard a noise and looked aroond, and who d'ye think was fighting?
I stood amazed and at them gazed to see them in such rages,
For I never seed a row like that between the Brockwell cages.

Wor old cage says, Come ower the gates because it's my intention
To let thee see whether thou or me is the best invention.
The new 'un being raised, took off his claithes, then at it they went dabbin'.
The blood was running down the skeets and past the weighman's cabin.

Wor old cage says, Let's have my claithes, thou thought that thou could flay me,
But if I'd been as young as thou I's certain I could pay thee.
The Patent knocked his ankle off and they both had cutten faces.
The shifters rapped through for to ride so they both went to their places.

When ganning up and down the shaft the Patent cage did threaten
For to take wor old 'un's life if they stopped it meetin'.
Wor old cage bawled out as they passed, Thou nasty, dirty Patent,
Rub thy eyes against the skeets, I think thou's hardly wakened.

The Patent to wor old cage says, Although I be a stranger,
I can work my work as weel as thou, and free the men frae danger.
Now if the rope should break with me, old skinny jaws, just watch
    us,
Thou'll see me clag on to the skeets for I's full of springs and
    catches.

Wor old cage to the Patent says, I warrant thou thinks thou's
    clever,
Because they've polished thou with paint, but thou'lt not last for
    ever.
The paint on thou'll wear away and then thou's lost thy beauty.
They never painted me at all and still I've done my duty.

The brakesman brought them both to bank the mischief for to
    settle,
They fit frae five o'clock to six and the Patent won the battle.
It took the brakesman half a shift to clag them up with plasters.
Wor old cage sent his notice in but just to vex the masters.

spoken: They're matched to fight again, but not under Queensberry
Rules. Wor old cage fancies fighting with the bare fist. I'll let ye
know when it comes off. It'll have to be kept quiet. If the Bobby
gets to know, they'll be both taken, because they will not allow
bare-fist fighting now. Keep on looking in the *Christian Herald* and
ye'll see when it comes off, and where. There's six to four on the
old 'un now. Bet nowt till the day, and I'll see ye in the field. It's a
cheet.

Tradition has it, locally, that Armstrong made this up the same day
he threw a charge of dynamite into the brazier by Joseph Badun,
alias Maiden Law Joe, immortalised in *Oakey's keeker* (q.v.). The
story of the old-style 'breakneck' cage fighting against the new-
fangled Patent in the boxing ring is a typical bit of pit daftness,
though in general the miners preferred the newer and safer means
of transport to the bottom of the shaft.

THE HASWELL CAGES

tune: *The wedding of Ballporeen*

Come__ all you good peo - ple and lis - ten a - while, I'll__ sing you a song that will cause you to smile, It__ is a-bout Has - well I mean for to sing, Con - cern - ing the new plan we start- ed last spring. And the ve - ry first thing I will men - tion, With - out a - ny ev - il in - ten - tion, It's con - cern - ing this new__ in - ven - tion, Of wind -ing up coals in a cage.__

Come all you good people and listen awhile,
I'll sing you a song that will cause you to smile.
It is about Haswell I mean for to sing,
Concerning the new plan we started last spring.
    And the very first thing I will mention,
    Without any evil intention,
    It's concerning this new invention
    Of winding up coals in a cage.

It was in eighteen hundred and thirtyeight
We began to prepare to make the shaft right,
We put in the conductors from bottom to top,
The materials were ready prepared at the top.
    From the top of the pit to the bottom:
    One hundred and fiftysix fathoms,
    And the distance you do think it nothing,
    You rise up so quickly in the cage.

Now considering the depth, it's surprising to say
The quantity of work we can draw in a day:
Five hundred and thirty tons of the best coal
In the space of twelve hours we can win up this hole,
    About fortyfive tons in an hour.
    And, viewers, overmen, and hewers,
    Our engines must have great power
    To run at such speed with the cage.

Then as soon as the tubs do come to the day,
To the weighing machine they are taken away,
Where two men are appointed there to attend
To see justice done between master and men.
    And when they leave the weighing machine, sir,
    Straightway they do go to the screen, sir,
    And the keeker does see that they're clean, sir,
    All the coals that come up in the cage.

I've wrought with the corves, I have wrought with the tubs,
I have wrought where the baskets come up by the lugs,
I have wrought by the dozen, I've wrought by the score,
But this curious contrivance I ne'er saw before.
    When we get in, they then pull the rapper,
    At the top it does make a great clatter,
    And the brakesmen they know what's the matter,
    And bring us away in a cage.

And when the bell rings and the top we approach
It oft puts me in mind of a new railway coach,

The number of passengers I cannot tell,
But she brings a great many I know very well.
>   But I wish they may not overload her,
>   And do some mischief on the road, sir.
>   Too much charge makes a cannon explode, sir,
>   And so will too much in a cage.

Now the young men and maids sometimes take a trip
Out to sea in fine weather aboard a steamship,
But if any be curious enough to engage
For a trip down below and a ride in our cage,
>   It would be a fine recreation
>   For to go down and view the low station.
>   I wish they may meet with no temptation
>   When they take a trip in our cage.

From one of the first broadsides printed by George Walker of Durham, this song reflects the new technology on several levels: the wealth of technical detail in the song itself, which had to be right or the colliers would refuse to buy the sheet, and the somewhat stilted sub-McGonagall style, typical of the broadsides and a direct outcome of the intervention of cheap printing into the folk process. Haswell is a colliery village in Co. Durham, about nine miles south of Sunderland. The reference to an explosion in the second part of the sixth verse is particularly poignant, for five years after the publication of this broadside 96 men were killed in an explosion in Haswell. The temptation mentioned in the last verse was a very real one rather than the 'vaudeville commonplace' Lloyd considers it, for until the employment of women was banned in Lord Ashley's Act of August 1842, Frederick Engels' report still stood: 'As to their sexual relations, men, women and children work in the mines, in many cases wholly naked, and in most cases nearly so, by reason of the prevailing heat, and the consequences in the dark, lonely mines may be imagined. The number of illegitimate children is here disproportionately large, and indicates what goes on among the half-savage population below ground . . . ' Indeed, after the Act women were still employed in many pits in defiance of the law.

THE BLANTYRE EXPLOSION

By Clyde's bon - nie banks as I sad - ly did wan - der, A - mong the pit - heaps as the eve - ning drew nigh, I spied a young wo - man all dressed in deep mour - ning, A weep - ing and wail - ing with ma - ny a sigh.

By Clyde's bonnie banks as I sadly did wander,
Among the pitheaps as the evening drew nigh,
I spied a young woman all dressed in deep mourning,
A-weeping and wailing with many a sigh.

I stepped up unto her and thus I addressed her,
Pray tell me the cause of your trouble and pain.
So sighing and sobbing at length she did answer,
Johnny Murphy kind sir was my true lover's name.

Twentyone years of age, full of youth and good looking,
To work down the mines of High Blantyre he came.
The wedding was fixed, all the guests were invited,
That calm summer's evening my Johnny was slain.

The explosion was heard, all the women and children,
With pale anxious faces, made haste to the mine.
When the truth was made known, the hills rang with their
        mourning:
Two hundred and ten young miners were slain.

Now husbands and wives and sweethearts and children
That Blantyre explosion they'll ne'er cease to mourn
And all you young miners who hear my sad story
Shed a tear for the victims who'll never return.

But the spring it will come and the wild flowers after
That bloom through its summer so lovely and fair.
I will gather me snowdrops, primroses and daisies,
Round my true lover's grave I will transplant them there.

'APPALLING COLLIERY ACCIDENT IN SCOTLAND: A fearful
Accident took place at Dixon's Pits, High Blantyre, eight miles
above Glasgow, on Monday, October 22nd, when it is supposed
that ABOVE TWO HUNDRED COLLIERS LOST THEIR LIVES'
— so reads the prose text above a broadside version of this song,
which is known, not only in Scotland, but also in the United
States, where there is also a mining district known as Blantyre, and
in Northern Ireland. The lovely last verse here is adapted from the
version sung to Robin Morton by John Maguire of Tonay-
drumallard, Co. Fermanagh, which John said he had learned in a
Blantyre pub in the 1920s from an old Highlander who had worked
a shift before the explosion. The song has been well popularised,
and recorded, by Ian Campbell, Ewan MacColl and A.L. Lloyd,
though of late the habit has grown up of adding a second strain to
the melody which I feel is quite superfluous.

THE DONIBRISTLE
MOSS MORAN DISASTER

On the twenty-sixth of Au-gust our fa-tal moss gave way, And though we tried our le-vel best, its course we could-n't stay. Ten pre - cious lives were there at stake, Who'll save them? was the cry We'll bring them to the sur-face or a-long with them we'll die!

On the twentysixth of August our fatal moss gave way,
And though we tried our level best, its course we couldn't stay.
Ten precious lives were there at stake, Who'll save them? was the cry,
We'll bring them to the surface or along with them we'll die.

There was Rattery and McDonald, Hynd and Paterson,
Too well they knew the danger and the risk they had to run.
They never stopped to count the cost. We'll save them, was the cry,
We'll bring them to the surface or along with them we'll die.

They stepped upon the cage, they were ready for the fray.
They all meant business as they belled themselves away.

Soon they reached the bottom, far from the light of day,
And went to search the workings, and Tom Rattery led the way.

They lost their lives, God help them, ah yes it was a fact,
Someone put in a stopping and they never did get back.
Was that not another blunder? My God, it was a sin,
To put a stopping where they did, it closed our heroes in.

First printed in *Coal,* this song commemorates the tragedy of
August 26, 1901, when four rescue workers were entombed along
with ten of the men they were trying to rescue, as a result of a
mistake by the management. Andrew Carnegie gave £100 each to
the dependents of the rescuemen. The tune, as sung by Mr J.
Ferguson of Markinch, Fife, in 1951, is one of the great family
headed by *Bogie's bonnie Belle.*

JOHNNY SNEDDON

As— I went out in sum - mer -
time all for to take the air_____ I
saw a hand - some maid – en down
by the riv - er clear. ____ She wept and
she la - ment - ed, and bit - ter -

ly   she   cried, _____   Say - ing My curse up - on   the

cru - el mine where John - ny   Sned- don   died. _____

As I went out in summertime all for to take the air,
I saw a handsome maiden down by the river clear.
She wept and she lamented, and bitterly she cried,
Saying, My curse upon the cruel mine where Johnny Sneddon
    died.

My love he was a collier lad, he wrought beneath the ground.
For modest, mild behaviour his equal can't be found.
His two bright eyes and yellow hair, his cheeks a rosy red,
But alas my handsome collier lad lies numbered with the dead.

Last night as I lay on my bed I fell into a dream,
I dreamed a voice came unto me and called me by my name,
Saying, Jeannie, lovely Jeannie, for me you need not mourn,
But the cruel stones do crush my bones and I'll never more
    return.

Early the next morning my dream was verified.
My neighbours all came rushing in, John Sneddon's dead, they
    cried.
As he was at his work last night the roof upon him fell,
To the grief and sorrow of my heart no mortal tongue can tell.

The day was set, the bands were met, and married we were to be,
My love and I we had agreed to sail to Americee
And for to make our fortune all on some foreign shore,
But alas my handsome collier lad shall now return no more.

Summer it will come again, all things they will seem gay,
And lovely lambs around their dams will fondly sport and play.
Other fair maids will have their joy but till death I'll constant
    mourn,
For alas my handsome collier lad shall never more return.

Come all you pretty fair maids, I hope you've lent an ear,
For the grief and sorrow of my heart is more than I can bear.
Once I loved a collier lad, and he loved me also,
But by a fatal accident he in his grave lies low.

The 'come-all-ye' is a form of ballad that seems to have originated in Ireland, though it was also much used in England. As *Johnny Seddon*, this ballad was collected from a collier of Irish descent in Chopwell, Co. Durham, with a somewhat different tune in 1953. Sam Henry collected a fuller version, with our melody, from Mrs Sara Morrow of Broughshane, Co. Antrim, who called it *My handsome collier lad.*

THE TRIMDON GRANGE EXPLOSION

by Thomas Armstrong

tune: *Go and leave me if you wish it*

Oh, let's not think of to-mor-row lest we dis-ap-poin-ted be,___ Our joys may turn to sor-row as___ we all may dai-ly see.___ To-day we may be strong and healthy but soon there comes a change,___ As we may see from th'ex-

plo - sion that has been at Trim - don Grange.

Oh let's not think of tomorrow lest we disappointed be,
Our joys may turn to sorrow as we all may daily see.
Today we may be strong and healthy but soon there comes a
    change,
As we may see from the explosion that has been at Trimdon
    Grange.

Men and boys left home that morning for to earn their daily
    bread,
Nor thought before that evening they'd be numbered with the
    dead.
Let's think of Mrs Burnett, once had sons but now has none —
By the Trimdon Grange explosion Joseph, George and James are
    gone.

February left behind it what will never be forgot,
Weeping widows, helpless children may be found in many a cot.
Now they ask if father's left them, and the mother hangs her
    head,
With a weeping widow's feelings tells the child its father's dead.

God protect the lonely widow and raise each drooping head,
Be a father to the orphans, never let them cry for bread.
Death will pay us all a visit, they have only gone before,
And we'll meet the Trimdon victims where explosions are no more.

A lovely elegy by the pitman bard. Seventy-four colliers were lost
in the explosion which occurred on February 16, 1882. Maureen
Craik sings it on Topic 12T122, an album of Tommy Armstrong's
songs.

THE GRESFORD DISASTER

You've heard of the Gresford disaster,
Of the terrible price that was paid.
Two hundred and sixty-five colliers were lost,
And three men of a rescue brigade.

It occurred in the month of September,
At three in the morning, that pit
Was wracked by a violent explosion
In the Dennis where gas lay so thick.

The gas in the Dennis deep section
Was heaped there like snow in a drift,
And many a man had to leave the coalface
Before he had worked out his shift.

Now a fortnight before the explosion
To the shotfirer Tomlinson cried,
If you fire that shot we'll be all blown to hell,
And no one can say that he lied.

The fireman's reports they are missing,
The records of forty-two days:
The colliery manager had them destroyed
To cover his criminal ways.

Down there in the dark they are lying,
They died for nine shillings a day,
They have worked out their shift and now they must lie
In the darkness until judgement day.

The Lord Mayor of London's collecting
To help out our children and wives.
The owners have sent some white lilies
To pay for the poor colliers' lives.

Farewell all our dear wives and children,
Farewell our old comrades as well,
Saying, Don't send your sons down the dark dreary pit,
They'll be damned like the sinners in hell.

I must confess I always doubted the authenticity of this song, about an explosion in a Wrexham pit in 1934, though I sang it to the tune recorded by Ewan MacColl on one of the first long-play collections of industrial ballads. The violence of its condemnation of the owners' hypocrisy was the sort of thing I'd like to believe miners could make up, but it all sounded too pat. However, when I heard the recording Alan Lomax made of Mrs A. Cosgrove of Newtongrange, Midlothian, singing virtually the same words as MacColl, though to a different (and I think superior) tune, all my doubts were dispelled. I understand the song is also known among the miners of Nova Scotia. MacColl sings it on Topic 12T104; Mrs Cosgrove can be heard on Topic 12T159.

OAKEY'S KEEKER

by Thomas Armstrong

Oh Oak-eys, oh Oak-eys what makes you so bad? 'Tis e-nough for to make all your work-men go mad, We should like ver-y well___ to know what you mean The___ way you go on from the pit to the screen. You treat us coal hew-ers just as you think fit, The wa-ges are small that are paid in the pit, But what we are ma-king we don't real-ly know

Since they sent us old Maid- en Law Joe.

Oh Oakeys, oh Oakeys, what makes you so bad?
It's enough for to make all your workmen go mad.
We should like very well to know what you mean,
The way you go on from the pit to the screen.
You treat us coal hewers just as you think fit,
The wages are small that are paid in the pit,
But what we are making we don't really know,
Since they sent us Old Maiden Law Joe.

This famous old keeker must not understand
How we are tormented with ramble and band.
The ramble comes down, after firing a shot,
Among the loose coals, and it cannot be got.
By the light of a candle it cannot be found —
Daylight is different from being underground.
If this old keeker would only think so
We would speak better of Old Maiden Law Joe.

To do his duty is nothing but right,
But in hurting coal hewers he takes a delight.
If he pleases the masters that's all he cares for,
Suppose that he hungers poor men to the door.
At half-past six in the morning he starts
To fill up the box, which is only two quarts:
If he gets the first tub, how pleased he will go
And say, That's a start for Old Maiden Law Joe.

He was at the Bank-foot, that's near to the Plain,
We wish he was only back there again.
While he was there, he was doing the same,
He must have been born without feeling or shame.
They say there's a medium in every case,
He's not a fit man to have such a place,
For he has no feeling for men that's below,
This hairy-faced rascal, Old Maiden Law Joe.

This Maiden Law tyrant does nothing but shout,
Who belongs to this tub? Because it's laid out.

He smacks his old lips, his old hands he will rub,
Because he has taken a poor man's tub.
Amongst the coal hewers how well he is known,
His hardness towards them he always has shown.
What makes him do it I really don't know,
Thou cruel imposter, Old Maiden Law Joe.

I hope all the screeners, as well as old Joe,
Will think of the men that are working below.
Perhaps in a pit they may never have been,
There's where the hardship may daily be seen.
How would they like it, if they knew what you made,
When the pay came and the money not paid?
I hope that the whiskers so quickly will grow
As to fill up the mouth of Old Maiden Law Joe.

Now, Joey Badun, you silly old man!
You have nearly done all the ill that you can.
With age your whiskers are quite turning grey,
I think it is time you were starting to pray.
I never did like to wish anyone harm
But I doubt you will go to a place where it's warm.
It's nothing but right to reap what you sow,
They'll burn your whiskers, Old Maiden Law Joe.

Now if you take ill and be confined to your bed
Do you think your masters will keep you with bread?
Do you think your masters will visit you then,
For all you have always imposed on the men?
For all you did for them their money to save,
If you were dead would they go to your grave?
Not one single step with your corpse will they go
Because it's that rascal, Old Maiden Law Joe.

Now, Mr Badun, I'm writing too long,
I hope you'll forgive if there's anything wrong.
When God calls upon you, what will you say?
Those tubs will be standing before you that day.
If the old Devil sees you, he'll give a great shout,
That's Oakeys' old keeker who laid the tubs out.
God will then say, Down to hell you must go,
If you are the keeker called Maiden Law Joe.

I cannot improve on A.L. Lloyd's notes to Tommy Gilfellon's
singing of this song on the album of Tommy Armstrong songs,

Topic 12T122: 'The keeker is the overseer whose job it was to keep tally of the number of tubs of coal each man fills. If the keeker felt there was too much stone among the coal he might disallow the tub, resulting in some loss of wage. When Tommy was working at Oakey's pit he had, on this account, many a bitter argument with the keeker Joseph Badun, called Maiden Law Joe. Eventually he wrote this song to pillory his bitter enemy. Also he blew him up by throwing some sticks of dynamite into a bucket fire that Maiden Law Joe was squatting at one frosty morning, but that is another story.' I got these words from a little paper-covered collection of 25 of Tommy's songs collected together by his son, W.H. 'Poety' Armstrong, and printed by Noel Wilson of Chester-le-Street in 1909.

GEORDIE BLACK

by Rowland Harrison

Oh my name is Geor - die Black I'm
get - ting ve - ry old I've hewed tons of coal in my
time And____ when____ I was young I could
eith - er put or hew Out of
oth - er lads I al - ways took the shine I'm____

gan - nin' down the hill I____ can - not use the pick, The

mas - ter has no pit - y on old

bones. I'm____ noo____ on the bank, I

pass my time a - way A - mong the

bits of lads with pick - ing out the stones. Oh, my

name is Geor - die Black, in my

time I've been a crack I've____

worked both in the Gus and in the

Bet - ty,____ And for coals up - on the Tyne out of

oth - ers wor took the shine And we

lick them all for ir - on down at Hawks' - s.

Oh, my name is Geordie Black, I'm getting very old,
I've hewed tons of coal in my time,
And when I was young I could either put or hew,
Out of other lads I always took the shine.
I'm gannin' down the hill, I cannot use the pick,
The master has no pity on old bones.
I'm noo on the bank, I pass my time away,
Among the bits of lads with picking out the stones.
chorus: Oh, my name is Geordie Black, in my time I've been a crack,
I've worked both in the Gus and in the Betty,
And for coals upon the Tyne out of others wor took the
shine,
And we lick them all for iron down at Hawks's.

When I was a bairn carried on my father's back,
He would take me away to the pit,
And getting in the cage and gannin' down below
'Twas enough to make a youngster take a fit.
To sit and keep a door, 'midst darkness and gloom,
Aye, many an hour by mysel',
And hear the awful shots that rumbled through the pit,
And lumps of roondy coal came down pell-mell.

I'll bid ye all good neet 'cause it's nearly time to lowse
And I hope I've tried to please you every one.
Young lads that's here the neet, mind, do the thing that's reet,
In this world that's the way to get along.
But here's success to trade, both on the Wear and Tyne,
I divn't like to see places slack.
For if wor pit lies idle, no wages comes today,
It grieves the heart of poor Geordie Black.

Originally written in 1872, this song of an old miner shows that redundancy isn't a new problem. I first heard this sung by Brian Clark of the Ian Campbell Folk Group, on Transatlantic TRA 123, to a rather plaintive traditional tune suggested by Dave Swarbrick, which sounded rather too sentimental for my taste. The tune given here is as recorded by that fine Tyneside band, the High Level Ranters, on Trailer record LER 2020, with something of a vaude-ville feel to it. Pete Elliott of Birtley has a somewhat similar melody.

THE BANKS OF THE DEE

Last Saturday night on the banks of the Dee
I met an old man, in distress I could see.
We sat down together and to me he did say,
I've lost my employment 'cause my hair has turned grey.

I am an old miner aged fifty and six,
If I could get lots I would raffle my picks,
I'd raffle them, sell them, I'd hoy them away,
For I can't get employment, my hair it's turned grey.

When I was a young chap I was just like the rest,
Each day in the pit I would give of my best.
When I had a loose place, I'd be filling all day,
Now at fifty and six my hair it's turned grey.

Last Wednesday night to the reckoning I went,
To the colliery office I went straight fornenst.
I'd just got my pay packet, I was walking away,
When they give us my notice, 'cause my hair it's turned grey.

Now all you young fellows, it's you that's to blame,
If you get good places you'll be filling the same,
If you get good prices you'll hew them away,
But you're sure to regret it when your hair it's turned grey.

I am an old miner aged fifty and six,
If I could get lots I would raffle my picks,
I'd raffle them, sell them, I'd hoy them away,
For I can't get employment, my hair it's turned grey.

From the singing of the late Jack Elliott on Leader LEA 4001. The song was originally communicated to the editor of *Coal* by Mr J. White of Houghton-le-Spring, Co. Durham, who added: 'To appreciate this song, it is necessary to understand the system of wage-basing in Durham County. If men earned more than 10 per cent over the county average, the owners could and did apply for a reduction in score, or tonnage rates, and thereby ensured that prices were never high.' Though this dates the song, it can't be as old as all that, for 100 years earlier a 56-year-old miner would be something of a rarity. As Frederick Engels said: '... the coal miners age early and become unfit for work soon after the fortieth year ... This applies to those who loosen the coal from the bed; the loaders, who have constantly to lift heavy blocks of coal into the tubs, age with the 28th or 30th year ...' Perhaps, in an earlier version, the old miner was aged thirty and six.

I COULD HEW

by Ed Pickford

When I was young and in my prime,
Ee, aye, I could hew.
Whey, I was hewing all the time.
Noo my hewing days are through, through,
Noo my hewing days are through.

At the face the dust did flee,
Ee, aye, I could hew,
But noo the dust is killing me.
Noo my hewing days are through, through,
Noo my hewing days are through.

I've lain doon flat and shovelled coal,
Ee, aye, I could hew.
My eyes did smart in the dust-filled hole.
Noo my hewing days are through, through,
Noo my hewing days are through.

I've worked with marrows and they were men,
Ee, aye, I could hew.

Whey, they were men and sons of men.
Noo my hewing days are through, through,
Noo my hewing days are through.

I know that work was made by men,
Ee, aye, I could hew.
But who made dust I'll never ken.
Noo my hewing days are through, through,
Noo my hewing days are through.

It's soon this put nae mair I'll see,
Ee, aye, I could hew.
But I'll carry it roond inside of me.
Noo my hewing days are through, through,
Noo my hewing days are through.

THE COAL OWNER
AND THE PITMAN'S WIFE

by William Hornsby

A dia-logue I'll tell you as true as my life. It's between a coal-ow-ner and a poor pit-man's wife. As
she was a tra-vel-ling all on the high-way, She
met a coal-ow-ner and this she did say: Der-ry
down, down, down der-ry down.

A dialogue I'll tell you as true as my life,
It's between a coalowner and a poor pitman's wife.
As she was a-travelling all on the highway,
She met a coalowner and this she did say,

chorus: Derry down, down, down derry down.

Good morning Lord Firedamp, this woman she said,
I'll do you no harm, sir, so don't be afraid.
If you'd been where I've been the most of my life
You wouldn't turn pale at a poor pitman's wife.

Then where do you come from? the owner he cries.
I come from hell the poor woman replies.
If you come from hell then come tell me quite plain
How you contriv-ed to get out again.

The way I got out, the truth I will tell,
They're turning the poor folk all out of hell,
This to make room for the rich wicked race
For there are a great number of them in that place.

And the coalowners is the next on command
To arrive in hell as I understand,
For I heard the old devil say as I came out
That the coalowners all had receiv-ed their rout.

Then how does the devil behave in that place?
Oh sir, he is cruel to that rich wicked race.
He is far more crueller than you can suppose,
Even like a mad bull with a ring through his nose.

If you be a coalowner sir, take my advice,
Agree with your men and give them a fair price,
For if and you do not, I know very well,
You will be in great danger of going to hell.

For all you coalowners great fortunes has made
By those jovial men that works in the coal trade.
Now how can you think for to prosper and thrive
By wanting to starve your poor workmen alive?

Good woman, says he, I must bid you farewell.
You give me a dismal account about hell.
If all this be true that you say unto me
I'll go home like a whippet, with my poor men agree.

So all you gay gentlemen with riches in store,
Take my advice and be good to the poor.
And if you do this all things will gan well,
And perhaps it will save you from going to hell.

So come ye poor pitmen and join heart and hand,
For when you're off work all trade's at a stand.
In the town of Newcastle all cry out amain,
Oh gin that the pits were at work once again.

Well, the pitgates are locked, little more I've to say,
I was turned out of my house on the thirteenth of May.
But it's now to conclude and I'll finish my song,
I hope you'll relieve me and let me carry on.

According to Mr J.S. Bell of Whiston, Lancs, who sent most of these words to be published in *Coal,* this song was probably composed by a Shotton Moor collier, William Hornsby by name, during the great Durham strike of 1844. The tune came from Mr J. Denison of Walker. The 'derry down' chorus indicates its antiquity and the tune is a relative of the stirring *Henry Martin.* Most songs with a 'derry down' refrain used to be fairly salacious, and it has been suggested that the words, now nonsense, originally had a sexual connotation. In our own time, such musical terms as jazz, rock and roll, and reggae, also had an amatory origin.

MINER'S LIFEGUARD

Min-er's life___ is like a sai-lor's,___ 'board a ship___ to cross the waves, Ev - ery day___ his life's in dan - ger___ Still he vent - ures, be-ing brave. Watch the

rocks, they're fall-ing dai-ly___ Care-less min-ers al-ways fail Keep your hands___ up-on your wag-es___ and your eyes___ up-on the scale. Un-ion min-ers___ stand to-geth-er,___ Do not heed___ the own-er's tale, Keep your hands___ up-on your wa-ges, And your eyes___ up-on the scale.

Miner's life is like a sailor's, 'board a ship to cross the waves,
Every day his life's in danger, still he ventures, being brave.
Watch the rocks, they're falling daily, careless miners always fail.
Keep your hands upon your wages and your eyes upon the scale.

chorus: Union miners stand together,
Do not heed the owners' tale.
Keep your hands upon your wages,
And your eyes upon the scale.

You've been docked and docked again boys, you've been loading
two for one.
What have you to show for working since your mining days begun?
Worn-out boots and worn out miners, and the children looking
pale.
Keep your hands upon your wages, and your eyes upon the scale.

Let no Union man be weakened by newspapers' false reports.
Be like sailors on the ocean trusting in their safe reports.

Let your lifeline be Jehovah, those who trust him never fail.
So keep your hands upon your wages, and your eyes upon the
    scale.

Soon this trouble will be over, Union men will have their rights,
After many years of danger, digging days and digging nights.
It's by honest work we labour, careless miners always fail.
Keep your hands upon your wages, and your eyes upon the scale.

In conclusion bear in memory, keep this password in your mind:
God provides for every worker when in Union they combine.
Stand like men and stand together, victory for you'll prevail.
Keep your hands upon your wages, and your eyes upon the scale.

The origin of this song is something of a mystery; though the tune
is derived from the Welsh hymn *Calon lan,* these words are virtually
unknown in Wales, but well-known in America. Lloyd has
suggested that it was made up in USA by Welsh immigrants.
Clearly, the words are strongly gospel-influenced: there is an old
song to the same tune that begins *Life is like a mountain railway,
sometimes up and sometimes down.* But then that line is somewhat
reminiscent of a song by Charles Dibdin, which goes *Life's like a
ship in constant motion, sometimes high and sometimes low.* On
the other hand, the form lends itself admirably to moral homilies:
a poem read by William Brown at the first Durham Miners' Gala in
1871 could be sung to the same tune:

> *Think what power lies within you, for what triumphs you are
> formed.*
> *Think, but not alone of living, like the horse from day to
> day.*
> *Think, but not alone of giving, health for self and soul for
> pay,*
> *Think, oh be machines no longer, engines made of flesh and
> blood.*
> *Thought will make you fresher, stronger, link you to the
> great and good.*
> *Thought is a wand of power, power to make oppression
> shrink.*
> *Grasp ye then the precious dower, poise it, wield it, work
> and think.*

It is for this reason that the CND marchers chose the same tune for
John Brunner's song, *The H-bombs' thunder* (see *The Cruel Wars,*
also in this series). The third and fourth verses here are from the
singing of Redd Sullivan, back in the days when both he and I were
part of John Hasted's folk and political road show.

BLACKLEG MINERS

Oh it's in the eve-ning aft-er dark The
black - leg min - ers gan to work With their
mole - skin trou - sers and their dir - ty shirt There
go the black - leg min - ers_____

Oh it's in the evening after dark
The blackleg miners gan to work,
With their moleskin trousers and their dirty shirt
        There go the blackleg miners.

They take their picks and down they go
To hew the coal that lies below
And there's not a woman in this town'row
        Will look at a blackleg miner.

Oh Delavel is a terrible place,
They rub wet clay in a blackleg's face,
And round the pitheaps they run a foot race
        To catch the blackleg miners.

Oh divn't gan near the Seghill mine,
Across the way they hang a line
To catch the throat and break the spine
        Of the dirty blackleg miners.

They'll take your tools and your duds as well
And throw them down in the pit of hell,
It's down you go and fare you well,
    You dirty blackleg miners.

So join the union while you may
And don't wait till your dying day
For that may not be very far away,
    You dirty blackleg miners.

During the great coal strike of 1844 Welsh, Irish and Cornish
workers were imported to Tyneside to help keep the pits working
and break the strike. The locals gave them short shrift, in ways that
make recent media coverage of industrial unrest look like the quiet
conversation of dons agreeing to differ by comparison. There was a
real pitched battle on August 15, and according to Fyne's *History
of the Northumberland and Durham Miners* there were 'great
numbers wounded and severely injured on both sides, but partly on
the part of the Welshmen. None, however, was killed.' The
historian obviously thought this worthy of remark. Louis Killen
recorded this on Topic 12T86, while the brilliant young Irish
singer, Terry Woods, sang it with the first manifestation of Steeleye
Span, the electric folk group, on RCA Victor SF 8113, a flawed
but in many ways remarkable record.

THE BEST DRESSED MAN OF SEGHILL

or

The pitman's reward for betraying his brethren.

tune: *The peeler and the goat*

Come all ye min - ers far and near and

let us all un - ite —— oh In bands of love — and

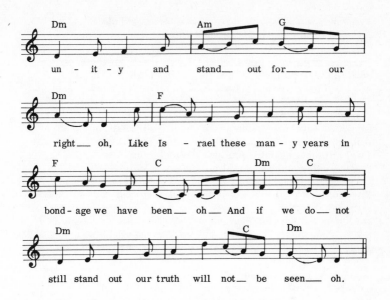

un - it - y and stand_ out for_ our
right_ oh, Like Is - rael these man - y years in
bond - age we have been_ oh_ And if we do_ not
still stand out our truth will not_ be seen_ oh.

Come all ye miners far and near and let us all unite, oh,
In bands of love and unity, and stand out for our right, oh.
Like Israel these many years in bondage we have been, oh,
And if we do not still stand out, our truth will not be seen, oh.

Man a weak frail being is and easy to deceive, oh,
And by a man called black J.R. was made for to believe, oh.
It was on March the nineteenth day, eighteenhundred and thirtyone,
    oh,
A man from Earsdon Colliery his brethren did abscond, oh.

And to the Seghill binding he did come with all his might, oh,
For to deceive his brethren dear he thought it was but right, oh.
But when he came to Seghill town the men were standing off, oh,
He thought that he would then be bound and he would make a
    scoff, oh.

As other men were standing off, he would not do the same, oh,
That idle work would never do, he'd rather bear the shame, oh.
Black J.R. made him believe that he was in no danger, oh,
And to the office he might go because he was a stranger, oh.

About the hour of two o'clock as I was sitting cobbling, oh,
A rout there came unto our house, I heard the women gobbling,
    oh.

Away I went with all my speed as hard as I could hie, oh,
To see if I could catch the hares, it was my will to try, oh.

But there were some upon the chase long ever I got there, oh,
With running so I lost my breath so I could run ne mair, oh.
But I will tell his troubles here as he came from the binding, oh.
They stripped him there of all his clothes and left his skin repining, oh.

Black J.R. was most to blame, but he lost all but his lining, oh,
And when he came to Hallowell his skin so bright was shining, oh.
They left him nothing on to hide that good old man the priest, oh,
But there they hung on him his hat, he was so finely dressed, oh.

They set him off from there with speed to an alehouse by the way,
    oh,
And there the Earsdon men did sit a-drinking on that day, oh.
But of their minds I cannot tell when they did see him coming, oh.
The priest he had within his hat and he was fast a-running, oh.

And all the way as he went home, by many was heard to say, oh,
That persuaded he had been to his loss upon that day, oh.
The Earsdon men they set him off from there to the machine, oh,
That stands upon the allotment hill, he there himself did screen,
    oh.

And there under a good whin-bush his priest and he sat lurking, oh,
I'll never go back to Seghill, but I will hide in Murton, oh.
And so remember, you that come unto Seghill to bind, oh,
You'd better think upon the man that we have tret so kind, oh.

Seghill was notorious for its short-way of dealing with blacklegs
(see *Blackleg miners*). This song is sometimes known as *The black
J.R.* It was printed as a broadside on Tyneside.

THE OAKEY STRIKE EVICTIONS

words: Thomas Armstrong
tune: *The pride of Petticoat Lane*

It was in Nov - em - ber and I ne - ver will for - get,___ The po - lice and the can - dy - men at Oa - key's hou - ses met___ John - ny the bell - man he was there,___ squin - ting roond a - boot,___ And he placed three men at ev - er - y house to turn the___ pit men oot Oh, what would I dae___ if I'd the pow - er my - sel'?___ I would hang the twen - ty can - dy - men

and Johnny whae carries the bell.

It was in November and I never will forget,
The police and the candymen at Oakey's houses met.
Johnny the bellman he was there, squinting roond aboot,
And he placed three men at every house to turn the pitmen oot.
chorus: Oh, what would I dae if I'd the power mysel'?
    I would hang the twenty candymen and Johnny whae
    carries the bell.

There they went frae hoose to hoose to put things on the road,
But mind they didn't hurt theirselves with lifting heavy loads.
Some would carry the poker oot, the fender, or the rake,
And if they lifted two at once, it was a great mistake.

Some of these dandy candymen was dressed up like a clown,
Some had hats without a flipe, and some without a crown.
Some had nae laps upon their coats, but there was one chap
    warse,
Every time he had to stoop, it was a laughable farce.

There was one chap had nae sleeves nor buttons upon his coat,
Another had bairn's hippin lapped aroond his throat.
One chap wore a pair of breeks that belonged to a boy,
One leg was a sort of tweed, the 'tother was corduroy.

Next there comes the maisters, I think they should think shame,
Depriving wives and families of a comfortable hame.
But when they shift frae where they live, I hope they'll gan tae
    hell,
Along with the twenty candymen and Johnny whae carries the
    bell.

Tradition has it that this song was written by Tommy Armstrong,
the redoubtable Tyneside bard, as part of a bardic 'cutting contest'
in the Red Roe public house in Tanfield. The subject set for the
contest was the situation of the men at Oakey Colliery in nearby
Annfield Plain, who had been evicted during the strike then in
progress. Tommy won, and this is the last we hear of his opponent,
one William McGuire. A candyman is a specially recruited bailiff.
In his *Northumberland Words*, R.O. Heslop explains: 'During the

great strike of 1884 men were served with notices of ejectment all round. To do this, the services of "vagrom men" were impressed. In these the pitmen recognised several as the itinerant vendors who called "Dandy-candy, three sticks a penny". Thus the term candy-man become generally applied in pit villages to those who served and carried out notices of ejectment'.

THE SOUTH MEDOMSLEY STRIKE

by Thomas Armstrong

If you're in - clined to hear a song I'll sing a verse or two, And when I's done you're going to say that ev - er- y word is true. The min-ers of South Me-dom-sley they ne - ver will for-get, Fi - sick and his tyr - an - ny and how they have been tret, For in the midst of dan - ger these har-dy sons did toil, For to earn their dai - ly bread so

far be-neath the soil, To make an hon - est liv - ing each min-er did con-trive, But ye shall hear how they were served in eight - een eight - y five, The miners at South Medomsley they're ganning to make some stew They're ganning to boil fat Postick and his dirt-y can-dy crew The mas-ters should have nowt but soup as long as they're a-live In mem-o - ry of their dirt- y trick in eight -een eight- y five.

If you're inclined to hear a song, I'll sing a verse or two,
And when I's done, you're going to say that every word is true.
The miners of South Medomsley they never will forget
Fisick and his tyranny and how they have been tret.
For in the midst of danger these hardy sons did toil,
For to earn their daily bread so far beneath the soil.
To make an honest living each miner did contrive
But ye shall hear how they were served in eighteen eightyfive.

chorus: The miners at South Medomsley, they're ganning to make
              some stew,
        They're ganning to boil fat Postick and his dirty candy
              crew.
        The masters should have nowt but soup as long as they're
              alive,
        In memory of their dirty trick in eighteen eightyfive.

Below the county average then the men was ten per cent
Yet Fisick, the unfeeling cur, he couldn't rest content.
A ten per cent reduction from the men he did demand,
But such a strong request as this the miners could not stand.
The notices was all served oot, and when they had expired
All the gear was brought to bank, the final shot was fired.
To hurt his honest working men, this low-lived man did strive,
He'll often rue for what he did in eighteen eightyfive.

Fisick was determined still more tyranny to show,
For to get some candymen he wandered to and fro.
He made his way to Consett, and he saw Postick, the bum.
He knew he liked such dirty jobs and he was sure to come.
Fisick told him what to do, where to gan and when.
So at the time appointed, Postick landed with his men.
With polises and candymen the place was all alive
All through the strike that Fisick caused in eighteen eightyfive.

Commander Postick gave the word, they started with their wark,
But they were done at five o'clock, they daresn't stop till dark.
And when they had done all they could, and finished for the day,
The bobbies guarded Postick and his dirty dogs away.
Fisick was a tyrant and the owners was the same,
For the turn oot of the strike, they were the men to blame.
Neither them nor Postick need expect they'll ever thrive
For what they did to Dipton men in eighteen eightyfive.

When Tommy Armstrong wrote this song about another wave of
strike evictions (see *The Oakey strike evictions*) he directed it to be
sung to the tune of *Castles in the air*, which he used for a number
of his ballads. But this lively music hall-ish tune is that sung by
Johnny Handle on Topic 12T122. I use it, in preference to
Armstrong's own choice, partly for variety's sake, but mainly
because I feel it fits the spirit of the text rather better. As Lloyd
has pointed out, most of the words Armstrong set to *Castles in the
air* were more solemn and literary than this vigorous piece of
invective.

THE DURHAM LOCK-OUT

words: Thomas Armstrong
tune: *Castles in the air*

In our Durham County I'm sorry for to say
That hunger and starvation is increasing every day,
For the want of food and coals we know not what to do,
But with your kind assistance we will stand the struggle through.

I need not state the reason why we have been brought so low,
The masters have behaved unkind, which everyone will know,
Because we won't lie down and let them treat us as they like,
To punish us they've stopped the pits and caused the present
      strike.

May every Durham colliery owner that is in the fault
Receive nine lashes with the rod and then be rubbed with salt,
May his back be thick with boils so that he may never sit,
And never burst until the wheels go round at every pit.

The pulley wheels have ceased to move which went so swift around,
The horses and the ponies too all brought from underground.
Our work is taken from us now, they care not if we die,
For they can eat the best of food, and drink the best when dry.

The miner and his wife too, each morning have to roam,
To seek for bread to feed the hungry little ones at home.
The flour barrel is empty now, their true and faithful friend,
Which makes the thousands wish today the strike was at an end.

We have done our very best as honest working men
To let the pits commence again, we've offered to them ten.
The offer they will not accept, they firmly do demand
Thirteen-and-a-half per cent, or let the collieries stand.

Let them stand or let them lie or do with them as they choose,
To give them thirteen-and-half we ever shall refuse.
They're always willing to receive but not inclined to give,
Very soon they won't allow a working man to live.

With tyranny and capital they never seem content,
Unless they are endeavouring to take from us per cent.
If it was due, what they request, we willingly would grant.
We know it's not, therefore we cannot give them what they want.

The miners of Northumberland we shall for ever praise
For being so kind in helping us these tyrannising days.
We thank the other counties too, that have been doing the same,
For every man who hears this song will know we're not to blame.

Fund-raising songs like this one are common in most industries,
many of them dating from the wars of attrition between masters
and men in the days before the State stepped in and started the
process of incorporating the trade unions into the superstructure of

the machinery of government. This one dates from 1892, when the Durham mineowners proposed a ten per cent reduction in wages, later increased to 13½ per cent after several weeks of struggle. The tune used, these days more easily recognised as *Come all ye tramps and hawkers* from the great song of that name popularised by the late Jimmy McBeath, crops up in many industrial contexts. The song is sung by that canny Tyneside lass, Maureen Craik, on a record of Armstrong's songs, Topic 12T122. Alas, since she got married, Maureen hasn't been heard singing much, a not uncommon occurrence among great singers of both sexes.

THE POUND-A-WEEK RISE

by Ed Pickford

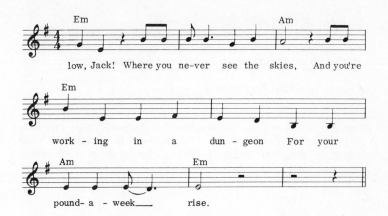

low, Jack! Where you ne-ver see the skies, And you're work - ing in a dun - geon For your pound- a - week___ rise.

Come all you colliers who work down the mine,
From Scotland to Southwich, from Teesdale to Tyne,
I'll sing you the song of the pound-a-week rise
And the men who were fooled by the Government lies.

chorus: So it's down you go, down below, Jack,
Where you never see the skies,
And you're working in a dungeon
For your pound-a-week rise.

In nineteen and sixty, not three years ago,
The mine-workers' leaders to Lord Robens did go,
Saying, We work very hard, every day we risk our lives,
And we ask you, here and now, for a pound-a-week rise.

Then up spoke Lord Robens and made this decree,
When the output rises, then with you I will agree
To raise up your wages and give to you fair pay,
For I was once a miner and worked hard in my day.

The miners they went home and they worked hard and well,
And their lungs filled with coal-dust in the bosom of Hell,
And the output rose by fifteen, eighteen per cent and more,
And when two years had passed and gone, it rose above a score.

So the mineworkers' leaders went to get their hard-won prize,
And to ask Lord Robens for the pound-a-week rise.
But Robens wouldn't give a pound, he wouldn't give ten bob,
He gave 'em seven-and-six and said, Now get back to your job.

So come all you colliers, take heed what I say,
Don't believe Lord Robens when he says he'll give fair pay.
He'll tell you to work and make the output rise
But you'll get pie-in-the-sky instead of a pound-a-week rise.

Pickford, a collier from Washington, Co. Durham, based this song on his own experiences in the negotiations with the National Coal Board in the mid-Sixties. I first published it in *Folk Music* magazine shortly afterwards.

FAREWELL TO THE COTIA

words: Jock Purdom
tune: traditional, adapted Jack Elliott

Ye brave bold men of 'Cot - ia, the time is draw - ing near, You'll have to change your lan - guage, lads, you'll have to change your beer, But leave your picks be - hind you,___ you'll ne'er need them a - gain, And_ off you go_ to

Not - ting-ham, join   Ro - bens'mer- ry   men.

Ye brave bold men of 'Cotia, the time is drawing near,
You'll have to change your language lads, you'll have to change
     your beer,
But leave your picks behind you, you'll ne'er need them again,
And off you go to Nottingham, join Robens' merry men.

Ye brave bold men of 'Cotia, the time is drawing near,
You'll have to change your lodgings lads, you'll have to change
     your beer,
But leave your picks behind you, you'll ne'er need them again,
And off you go to Nottingham, join Robens' merry men.

Ye brave bold men of 'Cotia, the time is drawing thus,
You'll have to change your banner lads and join the exodus,
But leave your cares behind you, your future has been planned,
And off you go to Nottingham to Robens' promised land.

Ye brave bold men of 'Cotia, to you I say farewell,
And somebody will someday the 'Cotia story tell,
But leave your cares behind you, the death knell has been tolled:
'Cotia was the colliery, her men were brave and bold.

For reasons forgotten by all the pitmen, the Harraton Colliery in
Co. Durham was always known as the 'Cotia, an abbreviation for
Nova Scotia. When it was closed as part of the National Coal
Board's 'rationalisation' schemes, the colliers were to be re-located
in Nottingham, disrupting families, drinking tastes, work patterns,
everything — all of them minor matters to bureaucrats with the
entire problems of a declining industry on their minds. Jock
Purdom, a deputy (charge hand) at the 'Cotia, wrote these verses of
farewell, and Jack Elliott of Birtley fitted the tune best-known as
Come all ye tramps and hawkers but more properly *Castles in the
air* to the words. Fittingly, for the great Geordie pit-bard Tommy
Armstrong used the same tune for a number of songs.

ACKNOWLEDGEMENTS

Although I do not accept a lot of their conclusions, it must be conceded that without the pioneer work of Ewan MacColl and A. L. Lloyd this collection would not only have been impossible, it would have been unthinkable. MacColl's *Shuttle and Cage*, first published by the Workers' Music Association in 1954, contained 21 songs, of which all but four were by industrial workers, the remainder being some of the first attempts by a contemporary poet to express what he felt were their hopes and aspirations, for the most part remarkably successfully. Some songs in both categories were recorded by MacColl as *Steam Whistle Ballads* for Topic (12T104). Even more remarkable than these was A. L. Lloyd's *Come All Ye Bold Miners* which Lawrence & Wishart published in 1952 and now, unaccountably, out of print. But many of the best songs, plus many others, were included by Lloyd in *Folk Song in England* (Lawrence & Wishart, 1967) which has now been reprinted as a paperback by Panther. Lloyd has also recorded an industrial LP, an album called *The Iron Muse* (Topic 12T86) on which he is joined by such excellent revival singers as Anne Briggs, Bob Davenport, Ray Fisher, Louis Killen, and Matt McGinn.

Among the other collections, still in print, which I have consulted are:

Frank Purslow: *The Wanton Seed* (EFDS);
Peggy Seeger & Ewan MacColl: *The Singing Island* (Mills);
R. V. Williams & A. L. Lloyd: *The Penguin Book of English Folk Songs;*
Alasdair Clayre: *100 Folk Songs and New Songs* (Wolfe);
Tony McCarthy: *Bawdy British Folk Songs* (Wolfe);
William Chappell: *Popular Music of Olden Time* (Dover reprint);
Ewan MacColl: *Personal Choice* (Hargail);
Frank Graham: *The Geordie Songbook* (Graham);
Gwen & Mary Polwarth: *North Country Songs* (Graham);
Joe Wilson Sings (Graham);
Sir Cuthbert Sharp: *The Bishoprick Garland* (Graham);
Stephen Sedley: *The Seeds of Love* (Essex);
Colm O Lochlainn: *Irish Street Ballads* (Three Candles);
Colm O Lochlainn: *More Irish Street Ballads* (Three Candles);
V. de Sola Pinto & A. E. Rodway: *The Common Muse*

(Penguin);

    Robin Morton: *Folksongs Sung in Ulster* (Mercier);

    John A. Brune: *The Roving Songster* (Cook);

    Eric Winter: *All Together Now — The Challenge Song Book* (YCL);

    James Reeves: *Idiom of the People* (Heinemann).

Thanks are due to Essex Music for permission to reproduce Ralph McTell's *Factory girl* also Mick Jagger & Keith Richard's *Factory girl,* to Robbins Music for Dave Goulder's *Turntable song,* to Lena Davis for Derrek White's *This afternoon's all mine,* to Ed Pickford for his *The pound-a-week rise* and *I could hew* and to Jim Ward for all his excellent songs.

I would like to thank the staff of various libraries in London, Bradford, Leeds, Manchester and Sheffield for their help in opening their archives to me, also to the staff of the Vaughan Williams Memorial Library at Cecil Sharp House, London and to Stewart S. Sanderson, director, and his staff at Leeds University's Institute of Dialect and Folk-Life Studies and especially to Tony Green whose forthcoming book we must all await with impatience.

Finally, without the invaluable work of Laka Koc and Gloria Dallas in transcribing the music the book never could have happened.

GLOSSARY

Ax — ask
Aye — still

Back-Shift — late afternoon shift
Bag — cavity in a coalmine, (verb) to sack
Bairn — child
Bait — food, miner's packed lunch
Bate — fine
Bellman — town crier
Bobby — policeman
Bout — without
Braw — smart, handsome, brave
Brawsen — gorged, burst
Breeks — breeches, trousers
Brid — bird
Bubble — to cry, weep
Busk — prepare, dress

Candyman — rag-and-bone man, bailiff
Canny — clever, handsome, trim, tidy
Cavil, Cavill — lot, share-out of work at coal-face
Chanty — pot, esp. chamber pot
Chiel — child, person, friend
Chummin (sometimes spelt tyum'un) — empty tub
Claes — clothes
Clag — to stick
Claith — cloth
Clam, Clem — starve
Clart — mud
Clarty — muddy
Cloot, Clout — cloth
Cop — reel of yarn spun on a spindle

Corve — curve, coal wagon, tub
Cropper — cloth shearer
Cuddy — donkey

Deputy — underground official over a district
Divn't — don't
Docken, Docking — dock, Rumex obtusifolius
Doffer — boy or girl who removes full bobbins and replaces by empty
Doup, Dowp — arse
Drift — underground passage, often used to ventilate or drain
Duds — clothes

Far End — end of one's resources
Fettle — condition, (verb) to repair
Firedamp — carburetted hydrogen, explosive gas
Flipe — brim of hat
Fornenst — opposite, alongside
Fratch — quarrel
Frowsy — unkempt

Gaffer — master, employer
Gallowa', Galloway — pit pony
Gan, Gang — go
Gannin Board — board for transporting coal from the workings
Gateside — Gateshead
Gey — very
Gin — if
Gowdie — golden
Gowk — cuckoo, fool
Gully — knife
Guttle — eat

Hackler, Heckler — dresser of flax or hemp
Hame (pronounced *hyem* on Tyneside) — home
Heid — head
Hinny — honey (affectionate), also short for SINGING HINNY
Hippin — napkin, diaper
Hitch — wrestling throw, broken coal near subsidence
Hogger — gaiter, purse, pumping pipe
Hoo — she
Howl kite — empty stomach
Hoy — throw

Inbye — in the workings, away from the shaft

246

Joss — foreman, boss
Jud — part of the seam ready for blasting

Keeker — overseer appointed to inspect coals as they come from
    the mine
Keel — flat-bottomed boat
Kemp — to compete, esp. reaping
Kelter — money, litter, nonsense, speed
Ken — know
Kent — knew
Kist — chest
Kittley, Kettley — ticklish

Limber — shafts of tub
Limmer — connection between pony harness and tub
Linderins — rope put round a weaver's beam when the weft is
    nearly finished
Lowe — light
Lowse — dismiss, leave (loose)
Lug — ear, hair

Marrow, Marra, Marrer — mate, equal, one of a pair
Mun — must

Nae — no
Neuk — nook, niche
Nobbut — nothing but, only
Noo — now
Nowt, Nowse — nothing

Over, Ower — too
Overman — underground official over several deputies
Owt — anything

Pincop — pirn, weft bobbin
Pinny — pinafore, apron
Poke — cover for wrapping warps
Powl — to leave work to drink
Put — to push
Putter — pusher, worker who moves tubs of coal from workings

Rapper — signal lever, boy working signal lever
Reet — right
Reyk — blow
Riving and tewing — pushing and pulling

Sair — sore, very badly
Sark — shirt
Scooper — coal wagon
Shifter — superintendent who allocates shifts, time worker rather than piece worker, worker by shift rather than by yard or ton
Shin-splint — leg protection
Singing hinnies, Spice hinnies (abbrev. hinnies) — girdle scones
Sneck, Snick — latch
Speel — fire, spark
Sprag — short pit-prop used when miner is under-cutting
Spyen, Spane — to wean, dry up the milk
String — 10ft length of cloth by which payment was reckoned, fault in cloth
Stow — to pack stone into hollows
Stroddle — stroll
Swally — small hole in the ground

Tae — to
Tarn — pool
Tazzling — tangled
Thrutch — thrust
Tram — coal wagon
Trapper — boy responsible for opening and closing trapdoor
Tret — treated
Trig — brisk, healthy
Tub — coal wagon
Tuner — loom engineer
Twine — spin, weave, twist

Wame — belly
Weel-faured — well-favoured
Weller — better
Welly — very
Whin-bush — furze-bush
Wick — quick, young
Wor — our, we

INDEX

Alphabetical Index to Titles (in capitals), first lines and choruses